by

Clare Lawrence

WITHDRAWN

Emerald Guides

www.straightforwardco.co.uk

Emerald Guides

ISBN
978-1-84716-726-2

Printed by 4edge www.4edge.co.uk

Cover design by Bookworks

"Autistic people have their place in the organism of the social community. They fulfil their role well, perhaps better than anyone else could, and we are talking of people who as children had the greatest difficulties and caused untold worries to their care-givers."
(Hans Asperger, 1944)
['Autistic Psychopathy in Childhood', translated Utta Frith, 1991, *Autism and Asperger syndrome.* Cambridge University Press.]

For Laurie

Explaining Autism

Note:

This book contains a number of examples of people with autism in various situations. In each example, although the situations are based on the experiences of a variety of people with autism, both observed and reported, the identities have been changed and details have been altered to make the example more universal. They are, therefore, designed to be illustrative, and should not be taken as direct case studies.

****

Preface to the second edition

As I come to update this book, I am struck more than ever with its futility: it really is impossible to 'explain' autism!

I know many people with autism – children, adults, women, men, people with jobs, people who are dependent on others, people who do not talk, people who never stop talking – and each is utterly different and totally unique. We may be a little closer to understanding some of the elements of autism, and in doing so be a little better able to understand the person with autism's perspective, but we should never presume to believe that we know what it is like to be that person.

There are autism experts. Each and every person with autism is an expert in what their autism means to them. We who seek to understand would do well to listen, to respect, to observe and to empathise. Understanding some of the elements which autism may include will help us in this, and that is where this book comes in. It is a starting point, a road-map to help signpost understanding. But it is only the beginning of the challenge and the joy of getting to know an autistic individual.

A note on that: many people prefer to use 'people first' language, and recommend that the term 'person with autism' be used. However, recent research (Kenny et al, 2016) suggests that the term 'autistic' is that favoured by the largest percentage of autistic adults. In this book I use both terms interchangeably. Also, regarding terminology, more astute readers will have noticed that the title of this second edition has changed from 'Explaining Autism Spectrum Disorder' to the more simple 'Explaining Autism'. Although the correct diagnostic term is that of a spectrum disorder, this feels unnecessarily clinical and negative to me. After all, need autism be, always, a disorder?

I hope you enjoy this book, and that it goes some way to opening the door for you into the fascinating, frustrating, intriguing and absorbing world that is autism. If you are reading it, the chances are that someone you care about is autistic. I hope this book goes some way to reassuring you that means you are in for an adventure, but that there is certainly plenty ahead to celebrate and to enjoy.

C.L., 2017.

Kenny, L., Hattersley, C., Molins, B., Buckley, C., Povey, C., & Pellicano, E. (2016). Which terms should be used to describe autism? Perspectives from the UK autism community. *Autism*, *20*(4), 442-462.

****

Introduction

This book sets about to try to give a brief and accessible introduction to – to 'explain' – autism. But why would most of us need autism explaining to us? Surely very few of us are ever going to know someone with autism, so why do we need to know?

According to Tian Zheng at the Department of Statistics, Columbia University [April 2009], we each of us know about 770 people at any one time. Conservative estimates of the prevalence of autism in the general population [Baird et al, 2006] are about one in a hundred, so (although this is an unscientific way of doing it!), each of us may be likely to know around seven people with autism at any one time in our lives. Of course, some of us will know a great many more than that if autism is our field or our interest or if it is in our family, and many will know fewer, but the point is that ALL of us are going to know SOME people with autism. We are going to meet them at work, as pupils in our child's class, as members of our golf club or choir or gym or book group. All of us could do with having a better understanding of what autism is, of what it means, of how we can make communication easier with and for people with autism and how we can be involved in making the general environment more welcoming.

So who is this book for? It is for parents of a child with autism, for grandparents, aunts and uncles, brothers and sisters. It is for friends, girlfriends and boyfriends, husbands and wives, for the person with autism himself and his own children. It is for the teacher and employer, for the person in the library, the policeman, the security guard and the dentist. It is for the person who fits shoes and the person who cuts hair – for anyone who will come across people with autism in their lives. In other words, it is for everyone.

Incidentally, I am referring to the person with autism as 'he' throughout this book, but that is not really fair. Although men may still be more likely to receive a diagnosis of autism than women, autism itself and the different way it presents is now being more widely recognised in girls and women. "Asperger's and Girls" (Tony Attwood et al, Dec. 2006) is an excellent resource that explores how autism may present in girls and women, and is well worth reading. For clarity in this book, however, unless I am using a particular example I will refer to the person with autism as 'he', and parents, teachers, carers etc., in the main as 'she'. It just makes the grammar easier!

Autism or Asperger syndrome? Introducing the spectrum.

Although the term autism is becoming more commonly used, it leaves many people confused. What is the 'Autism Spectrum'? Does it include Asperger syndrome, and what's the difference between autism and Asperger syndrome anyway?

The term 'autism spectrum' was first used by Lorna Wing and Judith Gould in 1979. It was used when it became understood that autism was not a single, separate condition but something that occurs on a continuum, from an extreme where the individual is considerably withdrawn and cut off from the rest of the world right through to the 'active but odd' person who may have a job, an education (often to a very high level), a family and all the usual trappings of an ordinary life, but who is known as slightly eccentric, different or unusual in his social interactions and relationships.

Since this spectrum has been recognised there has been a veritable flourish to identify and post-diagnose the famous throughout history with autism. Mozart, Einstein, Newton, Andy Warhol, George Orwell, Napoleon … all have been put forward at some time as autistic. The point of these speculations, I think, is the recognition that autism is not new, nor has the 'type' – unusual thinkers, people who see things differently, those who find ordinary social relationships difficult to manage or maintain – sprung into being since given a name. There is an ongoing and vociferous debate about whether autism is becoming more prevalent. Perhaps all that is happening is that we are getting more sophisticated in identifying the spectrum as more than a single, rather obvious condition.

Autism as a term was first used in 1911, and was adopted by Leo Kanner during his research in America in the 1940s. He described a condition called 'infantile autism' to describe a sub-group of his childhood schizophrenia study. At much the same time Hans Asperger in Austria was studying a group of children he described as having 'autistic psychopathy'. Kanner was writing in English and his work gained considerable attention in the English-speaking world, while Asperger's work remained confined to Europe and was not widely recognised until brought to attention by Lorna Wing in her research paper of 1981. Perhaps because of this, and perhaps because the war years in which they were working made communication difficult, Kanner's autism was widely known throughout the '50s and '60s where Hans Asperger's work has only really been acknowledged since the 1980s. Were each familiar with each other's work? Asperger read and acknowledged Kanner's work on Infantile Autism but it is not clear whether Kanner was aware of Asperger's writings. What is least clear of all is whether they were describing the same condition, or two different ones.

'Kanner's autism' (or 'Classic autism') came to be used as a term to refer to the condition as it affects people who have an additional learning difficulty (or, in other words, an IQ measured at below 70), with 'High Functioning Autism' used for people with an IQ in the 'normal' (70 – 130) range, or indeed above that. Since the condition as described by Asperger did not include learning impairment, and indeed Asperger himself noted that many individuals with the condition had superior intellectual ability, 'Asperger syndrome' began to be used to describe the intellectually able sub-section of the autism spectrum. However, many argued that they were simply the same condition by another name, and they became categorised as such in the diagnostic criteria of DSM-5, with the removal of Asperger syndrome as a separate diagnosis and the creation of Autism Spectrum Disorder as the umbrella term.

However, it is not as simple as that. Many people who received a diagnosis of Asperger syndrome (and have, therefore, a diagnosed pre-disposition towards sameness) prefer to retain the name. Other people reject the 'Disorder' element of ASD, arguing that 'Condition' is less judgemental, and therefore preferring the acronym ASC. Yet others retain the initials ASD, but take the 'D' to stand for 'Difficulty' or 'Difference' rather than 'Disorder'.

The terminology, then, just as the condition itself, is complicated, complex and varied. In this book I simply use the term autism.

****

Chapter One

What is Autism?

This is not a political book. It seeks to clarify, to explain autism to those who would like to know more. It is important, though, to bear in mind that although each of the following explanations for the autism spectrum focus on there being an 'impairment' or a 'weakness' or as 'unusual', that is not the whole story. Yes, there is a great deal that the person with autism finds difficult and problematic, but focussing only on the negative does no-one any good. There is also a great deal in autism to celebrate. As Temple Grandin once said, "If the autistic gene was eliminated at the dawn of time we would all be sitting in caves socialising" [Temple Grandin, *Thinking in Pictures*, 1995.]

The 'Triad of Impairment'

Although since the advent of DSM-5 it is less used, the 'triad of Impairment' was the basis of a description of autism for nearly forty years. The term was first used by Lorna Wing in her work, together with Judith Gould, in 1979. These impairments are in the areas of:

- Social Communication
- Social Interaction and
- Social Imagination

These three distinctions were tremendously useful over the years in defining the autism spectrum, and they made clear that the core element was 'social', which is why autism is seen as a social disorder (and not an intellectual, physical or mental one).

Social Communication

Social communication is the ability to communicate with other people. Most obviously this is done through speaking, although we communicate in many more ways than that. A look, a shrug, a grunt, a silence ... all may mean a great deal. It is only when we look closely at how humans communicate with each other that we realise how complicated the whole business is, and why having a difficulty understanding this 'language' might be such a problem,

Dillon follows the instruction to 'Knock and Wait' on the glass door of the optician's room, but does not respond when she beckons him to come in. She comes to the door and smiles, but Dillon does not smile back. She holds the door open, makes a further gesture with her hand towards a chair and asks him to "Take a seat". Dillon merely looks confused. The optician, becoming more abrupt now, commands Dillon , "Please sit down" and, since there are only two chairs in the room, Dillon sits in the nearer – and fortunately correct – one of these. The optician then illuminates the panel of letters in front of Dillon and asks him if he can read them from the top. Dillon answers "Yes", but is then silent.

There are many communication difficulties here for Dillon. He does not understand that a movement of the hand can mean either 'Come in' or 'Sit down'. He does not recognise that the lifting of the corners of the mouth is communication and demands a response. He takes literally the language of 'Take a seat' and is unable to understand what he is supposed to do. He answers honestly to the question about whether he can read the letters and does not see that this is in fact an invitation to do so aloud. What is important to note also is that communication is a two-way process. Much of what the optician does in the example is not understood by Dillon, but it is easy, also, to see how Dillon's actions could be misinterpreted by the optician. He may come across as unfriendly, stupid, ill-mannered or actively defiant, when none of these is the case. Misunderstood social communication is at the root of many autistic people's difficulties with the second part of the triad: Social Interaction.

Social Interaction

Many people with autism find being with other people very trying. It can be difficult to predict what the other person may want or do at the best of times, and if he or she is misreading your behaviour (as above), then it is even more confusing. It can be difficult to recognise, and even more difficult to understand, other people's emotions and feelings when they are not the same as your own. This can make social situations very challenging, and many situations from making a friend to attending a job interview, from sharing a table at school to going on a date may present huge obstacles.

Jay is waiting outside a lecture theatre. He sees a group of students from his tutor group and decides to join them. He goes and stands with the group, but rather than facing towards a point roughly at the centre of the five students, he positions himself facing, and very close to, one of the girls. She takes a step back, so Jay steps further forward. There is a silence. Jay stares at the girl's chin in order to avoid eye-contact, which he finds very difficult. "Did you know that the hairs that grow out of moles like yours are often much darker in colour than those that grow on other parts of the body?" he asks. At this point the lecture theatre doors are opened and Jay leaves abruptly in order to take his usual seat in the second row.

Although many people with autism do genuinely like to be alone, many others are desperate to make friends and to be included socially and are made very unhappy by their inability to be successful. Jay, in this example, is trying very hard and he gets lots of things right. He goes to join the group, he looks at least in the general direction of the girl's face, he introduces a topic of conversation relating to her, rather than monologuing about Japanese cartoons which is his favourite subject but which he knows does not interest everyone. He has understood the implied rule of the closed door and has not opened it and gone in, even though his watch says 11.32 and the lecture was due to start at half past.

What is so difficult for Jay is that virtually everything he does is, also, wrong. The subtleties of body position and angle are lost on him as are the implied discomfort of the step backwards, the inappropriate staring and (worse) the clumsiness of the chosen comment. Finally, he does not realise that a social interaction

18

needs some form of closure and to walk away abruptly is likely to be taken as rudeness. He comes across as pushy, rude, even aggressive or predatory when in fact he is just trying to manage that most difficult of social experiences, to 'chat'.

Social Imagination

The third element of the triad of impairment was the most misleading in its name. It seemed to imply that people with autism lack imagination, which is often very far from the truth. Indeed, the inner mental life of many people with autism is so strong and vivid that it can rival that of the 'real' world. What is meant by social imagination is the ability to imagine oneself into the mind of another person. It also involves imagining a situation other than that which is real and present, predicting not just what *will* happen but what *could* happen, and understanding that there might be a difference between the two. It is to do with imagining yourself into a situation in order to make sense of it, and with using an old or familiar situation held in the mind to interpret what is strange and new.

Marcus has a strong grasp of mathematics and is well aware that the probability of a double six being thrown by two dice is 1:36. When he sees an entertainer performing a trick that relies on a double six being thrown for its outcome, he is fascinated. He stays and watches the trick being performed again and again, each time a double six being thrown. His conclusion is that it is 'amazing' (because the probability is so slight, although possible), but he refuses to believe that there is any trickery involved. He accepts that the entertainer's performance relies on the double six, but he says that he is sure that the performer, who is engaging and friendly as part of his 'patter', would not use weighted dice. He fails to understand that, in the context of an entertainment show, this deceit would be not only probable but socially acceptable.

Marcus' gullibility is a trait too often observable in people with autism. For the person with autism, his very honesty can make him very vulnerable. He may be 'set up' by less honourable associates to do something that may get him into trouble at school, or even with the police. It also makes him poor at the 'white lie'. If you ask a person with autism, "Does my bum look big in this?", you should be prepared for an honest answer!

After the Triad

The new diagnostic criteria for autism do not use the triad. Instead the criteria are, in summary, 'significant, persistent deficits in social communication and interactions' and 'restricted, repetitive patterns of behaviour, interests, and activities' (DSM-5). For the first time, issues of sensory processing are also mentioned in the diagnostic criteria.

Unusual Sensory Processing

Differences in the way information from the senses is interpreted has become recognised as something that a great many people with autism experience.

These differences can occur right across the senses – in sight, smell, taste, touch and hearing, and in other senses such as

balance and recognising body messages such as hunger or thirst –
and can manifest themselves in too strong a sensitivity or as too
weak a sensitivity.

*Lucas is unable to work in one classroom at college because of the
'buzz' of the air conditioning system. To the other students this
noise is so faint as to be undetectable, but to Lucas it is
excruciating. He likens it (in the way it makes him feel) to the
noise of a fingernail being scraped down a blackboard, a noise
which he has read causes some distress in others but which causes
him no problems whatsoever.*

*Michael cannot bear the feeling of cloth on his legs. When he was
younger he caused his mother considerable embarrassment by
repeatedly removing his clothes in public (especially in the
supermarket), and he has never been able to tolerate tight or
restrictive clothing. He now, as an adult, chooses to wear shorts
whatever the weather, and never wears a coat that is heavy enough
to give a feeling of 'holding down' his arms.*

Greater understanding of sensory differences in people with
autism has led to a much greater acceptance that the environment
in which they live, learn and work may need to be adapted to
make things easier. For example, many people with autism are
particularly sensitive to the 'pulsing' of fluorescent lighting, and
for a child for whom this is an issue, a seat near a window and the
use of natural light can make a huge difference to his ability to
study in class. It is important to understand that this problem can
be either too strong a reaction (hyper-sensitivity) or too weak a

reaction (hypo-sensitivity), and that either can be present across different senses in the same person, or indeed in the same sense at different times. Awareness of the possibility of reduced sensitivity is particularly important if a person shows limited reaction to pain. As I have mentioned in a previous book, our son had an unravelled paper-clip (of all things!) spiked deep into his foot and didn't react. If someone cannot register pain or cannot feel that something is hot enough to burn, for example, clearly this has seriously implications for his safety. Hypo-sensitivity to taste may result in a craving for hot or spicy food, and hypersensitivity may result in a severely restricted diet. Some people with autism are particularly attracted to certain textures (remember to tell your son it is not polite to stroke that lady's lovely smooth tights on the bus!), or to certain smells. Pica (the eating of things that are not food) is found in some people with autism and may have a sensory cause. Clumsiness and lack of co-ordination may also have a root in an inability to interpret the messages coming to the brain from the muscles and/or inner ear.

Taking a break and allowing a chance to move about to awaken the senses and alert the brain can help many children – and not just those with autism – to learn better. Many babies find being wrapped tightly in bedclothes helps them to sleep. Many,students swear that loud music helps them to concentrate as does sucking sweets in exams (although this last may just be down to a sweet tooth!), and many of us have certain smells we find pleasing (coffee brewing, bacon frying, my daughter's hair...). The way the brain receives and interprets information from the senses, and the links between this and what is either pleasurable or uncomfortable, is a complex matter. It seems that for people with autism, the way it happens is often just slightly different to that of the typically developing population.

What is synaesthesia, and is it part of the autism spectrum?

Some people with autism do experience synaesthesia, but it is a separate condition experienced by people without autism as well. It is when the information from one of the senses is processed as being from one of the other senses. In this way a sound such as a person's name may be experienced as a taste or a smell can seem to have a certain sound. More commonly, certain numbers or letters of the alphabet may be perceived as 'being' a certain colour, so that, for example, four is red or a capital H is yellow.

Since those who have synaesthesia have it from birth, this way of perceiving the world is perfectly normal to them (and by many who have it, thoroughly celebrated). The problems come when a neuro-typical person fails to understand that a person with autism has synaesthesia. "My hand is green" might just mean "My hand is hurting", and the answer to "What is 2 times 2?" might indeed be "sausages", if the smell of sausages is that particular person's perception of the number four. We who are neuro-typical are quick to see something as being 'wrong' when it is perfectly possible that it is just being processed differently.

Incidentally (and this is not really connected except in so far as demonstrating how un-perceptive we who are neuro-typical can be!) it is important not to get so hung up with the autism in a person that you fail to see the obvious.

Sally, who is non-verbal and has a diagnosis of autism, was being observed doing a task matching certain bricks with certain boxes. When given a yellow brick she placed it in the yellow box. When given a blue brick she placed it in the blue box, but when given a red brick she placed that in the blue box too. She was given another blue brick – she put it in the red box. Her assessors spent some considerable time discussing this, trying to agree on her level of comprehension, her ability to follow verbal instructions, to what extent her refusal to file the bricks correctly could be described as defiant ... but it took the student on work experience from the local college to ask the obvious question: "Could she be red/blue colour blind?"

Sometimes all of us can 'fail to see the wood for the trees', which brings us nicely to weak central coherence.

Weak central coherence

This theory, first put forward by Uta Frith in the late 1980s, suggests that one aspect of autism is an inability to put together various pieces of information to make a greater sense. The person with autism may be very good at understanding all the details of a situation, but cannot put those details together to see the 'big picture'.

Stefan noticed that his brother had water coming out of his eyes, that his face was red and that his hands were clenched at his groin. He was even be able to describe, later, how the cricket ball hit with some force but he was unable to understand that his brother was in pain and objected when the game was cut short.

ness in central coherence may be part of the reason why
with autism may appear uncaring and self-centred.
may have difficulty in seeing that if your car has
whether it is the fuel tank or the starter motor that
ss interesting to you than either a) whether he can
ther he can give you a lift.

*..... with autism may listen to the neighbour's tale that
her central heating system has broken down and that she wishes
that she had electric heaters. He may even discuss the possible
causes of the breakdown in the system, or comment on how
expensive electrical heaters can be to heat a house – but unless his
neighbour asks outright whether he has a heater she could
borrow, she may spend a cold night.*

*Our son, when he was about five, announced that it is not
permitted to ride a black horse on a certain footpath. When we
looked we realised that the 'No Riding' sign was indeed a black
silhouette of a horse with a red line through it.*

Some of the person with autism's difficulty in making sense of
the world may be because of this weakness in central coherence.
He may find it difficult to integrate information, or to use the
context of a subject to conclude its meaning. Most neuro-typical
people are constantly making connections, trying to work out
meaning. Shown a candle, a plate and a red rose they will deduce
a romantic evening; for the person with autism a candle, a plate
and a rose are just a candle, a plate and a rose.

How can I help my student with autism do better in exams? I know that he knows the answers, but he never seems to get the right information down on paper.

This inability to 'see the big picture' may be part of the problem that many students with autism find in answering exam questions. The problem with many exam questions is that you are not only being asked to write what you know, but to leave out what you know but that is not relevant. You are being asked to pick through your knowledge and to put it down in a way that shows an argument, an opinion or an awareness of a certain viewpoint.

Daniel was faced with the exam task, 'With specific reference to how glacial influence affected the development of the coastline of Norway, discuss how physical geography may influence the evolution of a society's cultural development.' He knew a great deal about glaciers and spent the full 45 minutes describing how they are formed and how their movement can shape a valley. Unfortunately the marks were all in the second part of the question .

Rhiannon got 'stuck' on question 3 of her 20 question maths test and spent the remainder of the exam time trying to work it out, failing to get marks for the other questions which she could have completed with ease.

Faced with the essay question, "Did Stalin betray Lenin's legacy?, Eric answered with a single word, "Yes."

Many students with autism are far more challenged by exam technique than they are by the content of a syllabus. Absorbing facts may be easy for them, and many students with autism find memorising details and recalling them not only relatively easy but quite rewarding. Gaining marks in exams, though, is not the same as knowing the answer and this needs to be made very clear to these students.

Although all students need some advice and practice at the business of exam technique, the student with autism is likely to need considerably more than most. Some time will need to be spent with him in going through how the exam itself works. If possible, try to get hold of information material from previous years that has been sent out to the exam markers, and allow the student to study this to understand how the marks are awarded. At very least, make sure that the mark scheme (the allocation of marks per question) is made clear. Go through this together and devise some 'rules' for each paper: if a question allocation is two marks, there is no point in spending more than two minutes on it; if a question is allocated 20 marks you should spend at least twenty on it. Go through lots of questions asking not, "What is the answer?" but "Where are the marks for this answer?" Your autistic student needs to be helped to understand that doing exams is not really about knowledge or understanding, it is about playing the game.

Extreme Male Brain Theory
Professor Simon Barron-Cohen of Cambridge University put forward the 'Extreme Male Brain' theory for autism in 1999. Put

very simply, this theory is that the typical male human brain has developed to have a strong ability to systemise and the female brain has developed a strong ability to empathise. He suggests that the hunter-gatherer had to work out how to set traps and to remember which berries ripened where and when (both systemising skills) while the female brain was busy working out how other people felt and how to build and maintain a social position (empathising). His theory is that the extreme of the male-type brain (which he calls 'type S (systemising)' together with a reduction in elements of the female type brain (which he calls 'type E (empathising)' may result in autism.

Part of his theory, which gained a great deal of media attention when first proposed, is that an increase of the male hormone testosterone in the developing foetus may explain the presence of an S-type brain, and that it may also result in a rather longer than usual fourth finger. This was reported, rather glibly, as the idea that having a fourth (ring) finger longer than the index (pointing) finger could be a way of diagnosing autism. This has been received with some doubt but I must confess that in the small and very un-scientific study I have been carrying out with friends and acquaintances, it does seem rather true. I guess time will tell whether history validates the theory or not!

Why does my husband, who has autism, never remember our anniversary? I thought people with autism were supposed to be good at remembering dates.

The husband may, according to extreme male brain theory, be particularly good at remembering and noting dates (systemising) but not realise that it would make the wife happy if he acknowledged the date of the wedding each year with an expression of affection (empathising). While he may note the date, he may not realise that he should say so and, more importantly, that he should repeat what a happy day it was for him and how valuable his wife is to him etc. etc. He is like many men, only more so. He may believe that he has already told her that he loves her, and, since nothing has changed, why would he need to tell her again?

Executive functioning

Executive function [Duncan, 1986] is the term used to describe various processes which underlie purposeful behaviour, such as planning, focus of attention and memory. In other words, it is the ability to organise and plan, to sort out not only what needs doing, but what needs doing first, how it should be done and remembering what worked last time. There has been considerable attention paid to the role of executive function in autism, on how prevalent problems in this area may be and on what that may tell researchers about the ways that the brain works. For most of us, though, our interest in executive function is far more practical: how do executive functioning difficulties manifest themselves in the people with autism around us?

A person with autism, regardless of intellectual ability, may have considerable difficulty in 'getting things done'. This may be a very simple task, such as getting dressed, or a highly complex task such as managing the mortgage, but the underlying problem seems much the same: an inability to sort out what is important in a task from what is irrelevant, and a problem both getting started and knowing what to do after the first part of the activity has been achieved.

Jamie's mother is extremely frustrated that Jamie seems unable to tidy his bedroom. She tries giving him instructions ("Put your toys away", "Put your dirty laundry in the basket") but Jamie seems incapable of managing the task. Eventually she tries the strategy of doing the actual work, but getting Jamie to give the instructions. "Where does this go?" she asks, holding up a toy 'Bat-mobile'. Jamie is unable to decide. Is it a car, in which case it should go in the car box, or a character toy, in which case it should go on the shelf? Since he is unable to decide, Jamie can get no further with the task of tidying his room.

The good news is that impaired executive function is a very practical problem, and there are many strategies that can help people with autism (and those who live with them) to manage better. Of all the 'problems' of autism, this is the one that, arguably, is the easiest to get round, and the one for which it is most easy to provide support, and for the person with autism to learn how to overcome himself. It may well be, of course, that it is this overcoming strategy that people around him have noticed and have identified as 'autistic'. It is much easier to stay organised if, for example, you make yourself a rule that you always answer your emails first thing in the morning, or you always do your washing on a Wednesday. Although this kind of rigid adherence to routine may be seen by some as 'odd', or may wrongly cause concern as being anxiety behaviour, it can be a tremendous help to the person with autism in managing, organising and keeping on top of many of the demands of life.

Theory of Mind

People with autism are often referred to as having an impaired theory of mind. In this context, theory of mind is the ability to understand what is going on in someone else's head, and that their perspective, their understanding and their feelings may be different from your own.

This seems to need some understanding in a person of his own mind first. How do I know that I am happy? Can I understand that film in French? What do I believe about reincarnation? If a person can answer these questions, is he able to take the next step and understand that someone else may view things differently? Just because he is happy (the blue team is winning at football), does that mean that the person next to him with the red scarf will be happy? Just because he can understand the dialogue of the television programme, will his ten-year-old daughter be managing? Part of this understanding that others may view things differently is the key to respecting another person's sensibilities. You may believe that reincarnation is a load of hogwash, but is it polite (or kind, or socially acceptable) to say so in front of your devout Hindu house guest? See the example of Rachel overleaf.

Rachel did not know that her son Adam, who has autism, had been involved in an accident on his bike until the policeman called at the door. Her son had come in and gone straight to his room. The policeman was convinced that Adam must be hiding something, but in fact Adam had not realised that his mother was unaware of his accident. His description of the accident, when challenged, was bald and factual. Only after careful questioning did it become clear that Adam was knocked off his bike by a car driven by a fourteen-year-old. Adam did not realise this information needed to be given to the police since he had been aware that the boy was very young since the moment he first saw him.

This inability to see a situation 'through another's eyes' leads to considerable confusion for many people with autism. Often, a person will be unsure about what information is general and what is known only by himself. Similarly, he may assume that others share his physical condition, so that if he is wearing a warm coat he will be unaware that his grandmother, who is wearing only a thin cardigan, may be suffering from the cold.

Impaired Theory of Mind may make an individual with autism appear selfish when in fact he is only – in its truest sense – self-centred. He may be hungry and get himself something to eat, without wondering if anyone else may be hungry too. More dangerously, he may laugh when he sees the man trip over the dog (because he finds the incident funny), but not be aware that the man may be hurt or embarrassed or that laughter is likely to make the man very angry indeed.

Lawrence observed that his mother 'had water coming out of her eyes' when she received the news that a friend had died. When asked how he felt he replied that he was "happy because the new Lego catalogue has just come out." When his mother put her arms round him, seeking comfort, he allowed her to do so, and then added, "I expect you are pleased. You like Lego too."

This apparently unfeeling, 'autistic' behaviour can be very hard to take, especially from someone you love. What can make it easier is the understanding that it is not that the person with autism does not care how you are feeling; it is that he does not realise that how you are feeling is different to how he is feeling. He needs to be told in clear language. The reasons for your differing emotions need to be made explicit and (perhaps most important) what you would like him to do needs to be made plain. Perhaps the mother in the example above could have said to Lawrence, "I am very sad at this moment because someone I liked very much has died and I won't see her again. I miss her. I love you very much, and when I hug you I know that you are safe and warm and it makes me feel better. Please may I give you a hug?"

Lawrence may still not have understood why hugging him could make missing a dead friend any better (do any of us understand this, really?), but at least he would have known what the situation was and would have been given a behaviour that he could offer that was a 'right' one. Not knowing what to do, not even knowing that anything needed doing, meant that his behaviour previously appeared uncaring and cold when really it was just uncomprehending.

Theory of Mind is often tested through setting an 'appearance-reality' task. The person being tested is shown an easily identified box (a Smarties tube for example) and asked what he thinks is in the box. He is likely (quite correctly) to say "Smarties". He is then shown that in fact the tube contains something else – nails or crayons or small pieces of Lego, something that is definitely not Smarties. He is then asked what someone who is not in the room would think is in the tube. The correct answer, of course, is Smarties. However, a disproportionate number of people diagnosed with autism will say nails (or crayons, or Lego depending on what they saw) since they fail to grasp that information known to them is not shared by everyone. [Gopnik and Astington, 1988].

More complex still, impaired theory of mind in people with autism may be strongly linked to understanding of emotion. In the example at the beginning, our character who supports the blue team may be happy because his team is winning, and may not realise that his neighbour is unhappy because his team is losing. He will almost certainly struggle with the concept that his neighbour was happy before the match because he *believed* his team was going to win even though they went on to lose.

The idea that you can be influenced by something that is only in the mind, and that is not what actually happens is quite a sophisticated one. The mind is not the same as the brain. The brain may be able to calculate how likely it is that one team wins against another, using statistics, previous record, players injured etc. The mind may believe that a team will win against all the odds. In people with autism, the brain may be crystal clear and functioning to a quite remarkable standard. The mind, however, may be more fragile. It may be difficult for a person with autism to understand beliefs without evidence, hope even in the face of insurmountable odds, or to pretend that a banana is a telephone when he knows full well that it is a fruit.

****

Chapter Two

So What Does Autism Look Like?

By far the most common response when we say that our son has autism is disbelief. It seems that the general population continues to carry quite a firm image of what autism 'is' in its head, and our son does not meet it. This is not surprising. Most parents I meet at support groups who are struggling to get their heads around diagnosis say that their child has autism "only very mildly", and many people reject the diagnosis for some considerable time (some, indeed, for ever) because it does not fit their pre-conceived image of what it is to 'be autistic'.

Clearly the general public must have an image it does accept as 'autistic'. This, I suggest, is of someone who has a profound learning disability and is profoundly withdrawn. Let's look at these.

Yes, some people with a diagnosis of autism will have a learning disability, although the degree of this disability will vary. Not everyone with a learning disability, of course, will have autism (I know people with severe learning disabilities who are highly sociable, and highly socially motivated). If it is true, then, that not everyone with a learning disability has autism, and that not everyone who has autism has a learning disability, who, if any of these people, is profoundly withdrawn?

While some people with autism will present as being withdrawn and aloof, many others will not. Having a difficulty understanding social rules and expectations leads to differences in social approach, but these can be manifested through too much talking as well as too little, through staring as well as through avoiding eye contact, through unexpected contact as well as through physical withdrawal.

Nor is autism a manifestation of tortured genius, as popular perception such as created by the film 'Rain Man' (about someone who did not, in fact, have autism) would have us believe. Yes, some people with autism are exceptionally intelligent, and some people have isolated 'islands' of skills that seem to be developed beyond what would be expected. Some are brilliant at maths ... but other autistic people have trouble with even the basics. Some people with autism show skills in art or music; indeed 'perfect pitch' in music seems more prevalent in the autistic population than the general. However, some people with autism are tone deaf and seem to possess no creative impulse whatsoever. While it is true that a person with autism's strong focus on what interests him may lead to extreme knowledge about some subjects, often this is of no practical use, and often the information is discarded as the interest moves on.

Given that autism can manifest itself in so wide a way, isn't it difficult to say exactly what it is? The answer to this is both yes and no. Yes, it is difficult which is why the medical profession is working on refining diagnosis all the time. For a diagnosis to be valid it must be precise, and there must be scientifically accurate and repeatable tests to measure for a condition. Autism Spectrum Disorder has its range of tests and measures, and these are being refined and 'tweaked' as doctors become more sophisticated in answering the question of what autism 'is' from their medical viewpoint. Perhaps more importantly for most of us, though, the more time you spend around people who have a diagnosis, the more 'what autism is' becomes clear. It may be hard to pin down, but it is not really so hard to recognise (although it is imperative that we don't all go around 'self-diagnosing' family and friends: that way madness lies!)

The following section takes a look at the face of autism, and does its best to bring what autism actually look like (...and sound like) into slightly clearer focus.

Language

Since autism is, at least in part, a communication disorder and since most humans communicate at least much of what they say through speaking, it seems important to look at language in people with autism. Of course, communication is about more than just the spoken language, but nevertheless, the spoken language is pretty important.

A person with autism may not use spoken language at all. This is usually described as being 'non-verbal', and is in itself quite complex. Some children with autism never develop speech, but others begin to learn to talk but then seem to regress and 'lose their words', usually it seems around the age of about two years. However, even the person who uses no speech at all is likely to have some understanding of spoken language. Some people with autism clearly understand complex speech but communicate themselves via a communication devise (such as one with buttons for 'Yes' and 'No'.) Other people with no speech themselves communicate via picture cards. PECS (Picture Exchange Communication System) is a popular system for aiding communication for people with limited verbal skills. Other people with autism have speech, but do not use it to communicate. Some people can recite whole passages from favourite films, for example, but not actually use words to express anything to another person. This can be quite subtle.

Alfie seemed to develop language 'normally' in that he talked at the right age, but his parents realised gradually that he was either just repeating what he had heard (including on one occasion the complete news headlines!) or later, repeating what he had read (he learned to read very early and seemingly without any input from anyone). He could and did recite long passages about the doings of Thomas the Tank Engine, but wouldn't ask for anything, even his most basic needs. His parents had to remember to give him drinks as he wouldn't say he was thirsty and on occasion they forgot to give him a meal since he never said that he was hungry. He was a most undemanding small child ... which in itself was not 'normal'!

Some peculiarities in language development, then, are less obvious than no speech at all. A child with autism may make statements but not ask questions. Non-verbally this equates to pointing at an object that is wanted (e.g. a biscuit) but not pointing at something to share interest (e.g. pointing at a helicopter). In other words, the *intention* of what a person with autism says may be different to that of the typically developing person.

Some people with autism display echolalia, which is the repeating back of what is heard. Again, repeating is a perfectly normal way to develop language in children (you hold up the toy and say "ball" and the baby repeats "ball") but in people with autism it is more mechanical. Often a person with autism will not reverse a question into an answer (e.g. "Do you want some cake?" is repeated back as "Do you want some cake?", not rephrased as "I want some cake" or − more usually in the smaller child - "Want cake!") and there is more pronoun confusion than normal (using 'he' to refer to self etc.).

Given that there is considerable complexity about the way language develops as well as the content of what is said, it is easy to see why Speech and Language therapists are important both in screening for autism and working with those who have a diagnosis. Of course, most of us use language for a great deal more than just asking for a train ticket or ordering a pizza.

Talking to each other is the way most of us make and maintain relationships. We exchange pleasantries on the street, we ring each other for a chat, we text or post on social media. This social use of language (given that autism is a social disability) is likely to be impaired in a person with autism.

Tom was explicitly taught that when someone said to him, "Hello – how are you?" they were not really asking after his health and he should not give a graphic and accurate reply. When asked, "How are you?" by his head teacher he replied, "You are engaging in social interaction. I should tell you that I am well thank you even though I earlier caught my foreskin in my fly zipper." His carers decided that further work needed to be done in this area.

Many people with autism may have an extensive and impressive vocabulary. When speaking about their special interest, their tone may take on that of a lecturer, and they may be happy to continue with a monologue for some considerable time. This pleasure in talking to impart facts is not quite the same as most people's pleasure in talking to interact, although in both cases the important point is that it is a pleasure. The neuro-typical person seems to have learned that this right to talk about yourself or about what interests you needs to be earned, in an exchange, by reciprocal listening to the other person talk about his or her topic. In a 'good' conversation this will be more than just a turn-taking exercise. Person B will respond to person A, and his or her own input will elaborate upon the same topic. For the person with autism this skill may be lacking.

Perhaps as part of this, a person with autism may have a rather strange 'delivery'. In most neuro-typical people's speech, the voice modulates up and down, the meaning of the words being subtly changed by changes in pitch and emphasis. Thus "You're an idiot" can be a dire insult or an expression of real affection and "I won't be able to go *tomorrow*" means that the person still intends to make the trip. The person with autism may have a rather 'flat' tone, his voice remaining more or less at one level of pitch. Equally, the person with autism may raise or lower the pitch in his voice or apply emphasis at 'odd' times, and the neuro-typical person, who is predisposed to read meaning into this, may find this confusing. If there is more to communication than language, there is also more to language than mere words. There is a lot here to struggle with.

Of course, we don't even use words in a straightforward way. Many people use colourful language without even thinking about it. "Judy was swept away in a tidal wave of emotion." Swept where? Was she hurt? What did this emotion wave look like? Many people with autism will take language literally and be confused by metaphorical language. It can be hard to be 'on the ball' when you are sure you are not even playing a sport! Perhaps just because this business of using language is difficult, many people with autism find it difficult to express themselves, particularly under pressure. A person may be slow to respond to a question (and will be even slower if the question is repeated or, worse, rephrased since he will have to start again at working it out), and may seem to struggle to get words out.

Ahmed is a highly articulate speaker who has made his reputation lecturing on his specialised subject of solar flares. However, when asked if he would like tea or coffee he has a serious struggle to answer. He makes a number of false starts, lapses into silence and seems to get lost in the middle of what he is saying. In the end he replies merely, "I will have water."

Quite often having a conversation with someone with autism requires considerable detective work. He may not give you contextual clues (so he will begin by saying, "I took it over to her but she had already gone" ... leaving you to deduce who, what and where for yourself), and is unlikely to 'repair' a conversation that has gone wrong.

Cameron's favourite topic was Bionicles (a type of Lego toy) and he introduced this, and started a detailed description, when asked by his paediatrician what his interests were .Unfortunately, the doctor believed that he was talking about barnacles, and asked whether Cameron had seen any on a ship's hull. Although Cameron's only response was to pause for a second and then continue with his description, it was clear that he was disappointed that this 'clever man' he had been taken to see should be so dense!

This incident is typical of exchanges for people with autism. There is a 'language barrier' between them and the rest of us, and while we find much of what they say puzzling, the same is true in reverse.

Another difficulty can be not so much with what to say as with when. It may be that a person with autism finds it difficult to grasp the unwritten rules of when not to speak (so that he interrupts) and when he should do so (so that he 'misses his cue' in a conversation). This can be particularly difficult on the telephone when there are no other clues available, and many people with autism find using the telephone difficult. The telephone has its own set of social rules, too, and these can lead to endless confusion.

Charles' wife asked him to call her sister to ask what time she was going out. Charles dialled the number and said, "What time are you going out?" Fortunately, his sister-in-law, recognising his voice, was not offended by this lack of introductory 'patter'. She spoke for some time, Charles disconnected and then remained silent. When his wife asked him what her sister had said Charles was unable to answer since he could not remember the whole of the conversation. Only when asked specifically at what time his sister-in-law was going out was he able to say.

Milo liked to answer the family telephone and had been taught a good range of answering phrases, and sounded most confident. Unfortunately, if asked "Is your mother there?" he would answer truthfully (either "yes" or "no") and would hang up regardless. Only if asked, "May I speak to your mother?" would he go to fetch her.

The directness of language used by a person with autism may, unfortunately, be taken for abruptness or even rudeness, when no offence was intended. He may be distressingly truthful ("Your teeth are yellow"). He may even appear confrontational, perhaps finding it difficult to refrain from pointing out when someone is breaking the rules. He may be the one to tell his fellow traveller that he shouldn't have his feet up on the seats, or the youth that it is not permitted to smoke on the train platform. In school, the pupil with autism may feel it necessary to point out when another is, or has, broken the rules and this clearly has a consequence for his acceptance by his peers. Although it perhaps shouldn't be the case, there is a necessary skill in knowing when rules can and even should be broken. Sometimes this is necessary just to 'fit in' and sometimes it is more urgent. There is a difference between the rules 'Not to be used by students' and 'Not to be used in case of fire' on a college door. In the first, if the building is on fire then the rule can be ignored. In the second, even in a fire, it mustn't be.

This 'failing to adapt' can often be noted in the language of a person with autism. Most neuro-typical people vary their language use in a million subtle ways, depending on to whom they are speaking, what message they want to convey and on how they are feeling. This altering of 'register' can be difficult for a person with autism who struggles with language processing. Often he may find that it is safest to be polite, even formal. Usually this a fairly effective strategy, although it works less well for the young person than for the adult. Other children are likely to reject an over-formal, over-polite contemporary who does not conform to the language and speech patterns of his peers. Even as an adult it has its drawbacks as sometimes excessive politeness can be taken as sarcasm or aggression when its use is inappropriate.

Jules wants to buy a bunch of bananas. The stall holder and another customer are engaged in a furious row over the fact that the customer claims he had been short changed. Since the argument is nothing to do with him, and since it seems that the previous transaction has been completed, Jules steps between the two and says, "Excuse me, I would like to purchase these bananas. I believe they cost £1.20." This is taken by the stall-holder to mean "I know how much they are so don't try to short-change me" and by the previous customer to mean "I can do maths and only a stupid person would not know how much change he should get", but in fact it simply means that Jules would like to buy some bananas.

Neologism

It is important to remember (and to keep on remembering, and indeed saying!) that not all of what is associated with having autism is bad. Having a condition on the autism spectrum can make life difficult for the person for all the reasons given in this book, but it can also be a source of richness, of originality and creativity. One example of this is Neologism.

Neologism is the invention of new words, or the use of words that have a meaning to the person who uses them that is independent of their common meaning. Of course, many younger children without autism do this, and not all people with autism, children or adults, will do so, but for some it is a particularly interesting and often creative trait.

While many children use neologism as they develop language, children with autism may be more likely to do so, be more likely to use words that are truly 'new' (and not merely mispronounced or misunderstood) and are more likely to continue to use neologisms into adulthood. According to some research ['*Neologisms and idiosyncratic language in autistic speakers*'

Volden J and Lord C; J Autism Dev Disord 1991 Jun; 21 (2): 109-30], "Autistic subjects were more likely to use words ... that have no phonological or semantic similarity to the intended English word." This 'creation' of language may be seen as more that just a failure to grasp the language used by people around them. Indeed, the frequency of this idiosyncratic use of language seems to increase with the users language ability and intelligence. The highly verbal, highly articulate child (or adult) with autism may use language in a most inventive and original way.

Some examples from a child with autism of this kind of use of language include using new words for a familiar object (calling a yoghurt a 'Rar'); creating new words for things that otherwise don't have a name ('Wootie' for the bits of fluff on the carpet); putting together combinations of real words to replace another word (calling an ice-cream cone a 'biscuit bag'); using familiar words in a way unconnected with the new meaning (calling a particular bag a 'will-power'); putting together new combinations of words to be used as given names (naming a tortoise 'Pull-Yourself-Together' or a popper toy 'Scary-For-What-He-Can-Do') and using words which make logical sense to the speaker but have no meaning to the listener (using 'Pocking' to describe playing on the computer.)

Although these idiosyncrasies can be a barrier to understanding (it is no use asking at school if you can 'pock' if you hope to be understood), they can also be rich and interesting. This playing with language, using the native language almost as a foreign one, may be strange but it can be fascinating. I have a friend with autism who can talk backwards – not just reordering the words but reversing the sounds of the words so that "hello, I'm pleased to meet you" sounds like "ooya teem ot desalp miooleh!" While this may not serve any useful purpose, and certainly hasn't helped him to find either successful employment or adequate support in the community, it is tremendous fun – and a better life for people with autism definitely includes having more fun, amusement and downright enjoyment.

Eye Contact

One of the more common observable traits of a person with autism (although by no means universal) is lack of eye-contact. Many people with autism report that looking into another person's eyes is distracting and makes it difficult to process what is being said. Others report that it is so uncomfortable as to be actually painful. An insistence to "look at me" from a teacher or other authority figure can lead to reduced ability to function and to great distress for a person with autism. Is eye contact really so important?

Marcus will stare at a speaker such as a teacher while that person is talking generally and until that person looks at him. If he is asked a direct question he will immediately drop his gaze or even physically turn away. He can only answer if able to stare at something 'neutral' (e.g. at a wall or at the ground). Now that his teachers accept that this is the case he is doing well in school, where earlier he was in constant trouble and was believed to be evasive and untrustworthy.

It is unfortunate that our European culture places such emphasis on the direct gaze. In some cultures it is more polite to lower the gaze, and presumably this element of having autism is less of a problem in these places. For most of the West, lack of eye contact may be taken as shifty and dishonest, and Marcus is not alone in being considered untrustworthy just because of his lack of direct gaze. A person with autism can be helped by advice such as to look at the bridge of a person's nose, or to look at a speaker's mouth. Without eye-contact it can be difficult to know who you are speaking to, so advice that the words need to be sent in the right direction (i.e. Send your words towards the ears of the person you are speaking to) can be helpful, as can the advice to watch words you want to understand as they come out of a person's mouth. Beyond this, though, no-one should insist on eye contact if it is uncomfortable. Like most things, if it is hurting no-one else why shouldn't a person with autism look wherever he chooses? He (presumably) knows what is most comfortable for him and what helps him to process conversation most effectively.

Gaze direction has more to it, though, than just whether or not to make eye-contact. For some people with autism, the idea that it is often necessary to share gaze direction with another person can be confusing. If I am making small-talk about the weather, it is quite probable that I will look towards a window (even if I have just returned from a ten mile walk and know full well that it is raining!) The person I am talking to, in acknowledgement of sharing that piece of small talk, will look towards the window too, and the two of us may well stand there gazing out of the glass as we discuss the dreadful summer. Not to share this direction of gaze may well feel uncomfortable. A person with autism who has been told to look towards the person who is speaking to him may do so to an excessive extent, and not pick up the 'now-it-is-time-to-look-towards-the-window' cues. Looking at another person may well be taken as an aggressive act, and it is important that well-meaning neuro-typical teachers do not make life even more difficult for the person with autism by making these rules.

Two young men on the underground were engaged in an increasingly violent argument. The other passengers all looked down or away as they did not want to get involved, but David, who has autism, did not. When one of the young man realised this he turned to David with "What are you staring at?". David continued to make eye-contact and replied, "I am watching you." When asked at the police station why he had hit David, the young man said that David had 'asked for it' and that he had been 'looking for trouble'.

Not all people with autism find the business of where to look difficult, but it is certainly not uncommon. It is important not to misread eye-direction in people with autism and to be consciously aware of how that person's eye-direction may be affecting you. It is easy to feel that someone who will not look at you must be lying, not listening or may just not like you and it is easy to take too direct a gaze as a threat or a challenge. Similarly, if the person you are talking to seems uncomfortable by your direct stare, it is a simple matter to look away. We are all communicating all of the time through our eyes – even when we don't mean to. Perhaps we should 'watch where we look' in the same way we might 'watch what we say' ... which is in itself a challenging statement for a person with autism!

Special interests

One of the more striking characteristics of many people who have autism is their powerful and often unusual interest in a topic. It seems that when a person with autism becomes interested in something, he tends to become REALLY interested!

Initially, for the people living with the person with autism, this can be a real problem as the person's interest over-rides everything else. If all your daughter wants to do is to collect tin-openers, to catalogue types of street lamp or to visit the locations of supposed UFO sightings, this can seriously interfere with your normal daily life ... and can drive you totally nuts!

There are various ways to approach this. One is to recognise what a tremendous asset this special interest can be. If someone with autism develops a particularly strong interest in something, this can be a tremendous source of pleasure, satisfaction and relaxation to that person and, coincidentally, can be a tremendous source of motivation. Most of us are motivated by reward, whether that be a sticker on a chart, a word of praise or a pay-rise. For the individual with autism, a chance to spend time on a special interest can be one of the strongest motivators of all, and acceptance of this is a vital step in helping that individual to learn and achieve. If a child with autism has a fascination with spaceships, she is far more likely to 'learn' if dealing with her interest. This might be as simple as using spaceship tokens to learn to count or it might be as complex as working out how many light years it would take a certain ship travelling at a certain speed to reach Pluto. It might be about choosing an early reader about an astronaut to teach reading or as complex as inspiring a story, a newspaper article, a formal letter, a poem or a book review on the subject of space. What is more, she may well know a great deal more about her special interest than any other child, perhaps any adult, in the school.

Appreciating and valuing that knowledge can go a long way towards preserving self-esteem.

Sumatra, a six year old girl with autism, had an over-riding fascination with washing machines. Her mother had to run the machine during the day, while she was at school, as if she put it on during the night even if Sumatra were fast asleep she would immediately wake and come down to watch it throughout its cycle.

Sumatra had eating difficulties to a point where doctors were involved to help keep her weight up to an acceptable level. Her mother had discovered that Sumatra would eat far more readily if sat on the floor near the washing machine, but worried that to allow her to do so was somehow not really dealing with the issue. The 'problem' of Sumatra's washing machine special interest stopped being a problem when all her carers learned to use this interest in a positive way. Access to the washing machine was used as a motivator for Sumatra. After initially being allowed to eat by the machine, she was gradually encouraged (over many steps) to start at the table and to move to the machine for pudding, and then just for a treat after dinner. A picture of the machine was placed after a sign for 'work' on her daily schedule, and a visit to the machine became a valued and valid reward. Sumatra's mother and other carers never understood what it was about the machines that pleased Sumatra. It may have been the spinning or perhaps the sound, the fall of the clothes from the top of the drum or perhaps the sequence of lights and numbers ... but understanding, or sharing, Sumatra's interest were not necessary.

What was needed was for Sumatra's carers to accept her interest, even without understanding it, and to work with her on using it as a motivator for other aspects of life.

Nor is a tendency towards having a special interest only a childhood trait in people with autism. The difference is that an adult is usually far more able to follow his interests without anyone else's permission. In an ideal world a special interest can turn into a job or profession, and many of our top mathematicians and science researchers might well confess to an almost obsessive interest in their subject if pushed! So might many of our most successful musicians, artists and writers. When a special interest (whether autistic or otherwise) becomes 'successful', it is seldom seen as a problem - who would dream of questioning Nick Park's continued interest in playing with plasticine?

Many adults with autism do not, of course, manage to turn their interests into successes in this way. For them, interests remain just that — but even so can provide a huge source of relief and pleasure. It does not matter what that interest might be (unless it is one that leads the individual into danger or that is socially unacceptable). Who is anyone to say that one interest is 'worth more' than any other? Nor need special interests lead to social isolation. The internet means that the individual with almost any particular enthusiasm can share it with an on-line community. Just because many of us may not share an interest in electricity pylons, does not mean that the Pylon Appreciation Society does not exist (see www.pylons.org for more information).

However, it should be said that for those of us who live with a person with autism some boundaries around the special interest can help enormously. The parent of the child with an interest in dinosaurs can limit the time spent being 'lectured' on the subject, while still accepting that this is communication of a kind. A deal can be struck that works for both parties: "You can tell me about dinosaurs in the car but when we get to the park we are going to talk about other things." Adult partners are often old hands at this kind of negotiation.

Maureen is used to having her holiday destinations decided by the locations of the grave-sites of famous composers. She has learned to accept her husband's profound interest in visiting these, and has realised that his interest frees her up to pursue her own interest in architecture. She has negotiated with her husband that they spend at least some days together on neutral pursuits, and on the other days that both she and he accept that the other person does not share their interest. On these days they still enjoy their meals together on the holiday evening as long as both remember not to go on too much about what they have been doing!

When does a 'Special Interest' become an obsession, and how can we help to control it?

Carers may become concerned about the extent to which a person with autism's special interest is taking over his or her life. In this context the special interest may be seen as being closer to an obsession, and as such be seen as a problem.

It is worth noting that seeing a special interest as a problem is a neuro-typical trait: it is very unlikely that a person with autism would see their interest as a problem except in so far as not being able to follow it for enough hours of the day!

An 'obsession' is something that takes over a person's thoughts and time, to the exclusion of other interests. The term is negative, and there is also implied within it a feeling that the obsession is unhealthy both in itself and perhaps in its cause. An obsession with home security, for example, may well be an outward sign of inner anxiety, and the obsessive need to repeatedly lock and check doors and windows may well have a negative effect on someone's life. It is important, I think, to differentiate between this kind of 'obsession' and a person with autism's 'special interest'. The special interest can be understood as something *wanted* to do — and something which is a source of pleasure and fulfilment and often social inclusion as well as relaxation and self-care — where an obsession has become something that the person feels that he *must* do, even when doing it brings only further distress.

These definitions are, of course, blurred. When under stress, many individuals with autism will increase their activity around their special interest as a way of self-calming and of coping generally. At the same time, stress is likely to increase incidence of obsessive behaviour, and it can be very difficult for the onlooker or carer to tell the difference. Perhaps what is most important to bear in mind is that in both cases it is the cause of stress which needs to be addressed rather than either the obsessive or special interest behaviour.

'Controlling' a special interest is another matter. It is probably true that, left to his own devices, an individual with autism might well spend all of his time on a special interest, with a result that he might not eat, wash, leave the house or interact with anyone else whatsoever. Although an adult with autism remains an adult and has the right to behave as he wishes, it can perhaps be argued that some intervention in this case may be for the individual's good. Certainly if the person is still a child it may be necessary to control access to the special interest if there is to be opportunity made for all of the other learning that should be taking place.

Perhaps the ideal is to strike a balance. If as parent or teacher, you are able to understand and use the person's special interest to motivate interest in learning and as a reward, both are likely to be very helpful. If you want your child to sit at the table to eat, using a 'Thomas the Tank Engine' plate may well be a good idea. Similarly, although your other children may understand that a clean plate means a chance to watch television, if your child with autism would be more motivated by the chance to spend half an hour downloading pictures of insects, then why not? However, he will need a time-limit set for when bug investigation must be paused and joining back in with the family encouraged. We can none of us do what we want to do all of the time (sadly!), and that in itself is a lesson that many people with autism (including many adults) may need help to learn and to keep on learning.

Sameness and routine

For many people with autism always doing things the same way and having a reliable routine are part of being happy. Much of this may have originated from learning to manage impaired Executive Functioning, and quite often what seems to be an inflexible approach may in fact be a reliable coping mechanism. When the world seems chaotic, making rules and having strategies that bring order can be a tremendous help. A person with autism may have developed a routine for leaving the house that includes checking each of the electric sockets in the house in turn, turning the electric oven switch on and then off, checking each of the windows, opening and then locking and then testing the back door and going out through the front door, locking it and then testing it. All of this may seem restrictive to another person, who only sees the time that the routine takes up. What the neuro-typical onlooker does not see is how hugely reduced the person with autism's anxiety is now that he has this routine in place. It may well be that in previous times he was unable to leave the house at all as he could not be sure 'what needed doing' in order to leave it safely. He has now worked out a routine that enables him to check each of the problem areas, and means that he can leave the house confident that all is safe. Similarly, he may only be willing to park if a space is available in a certain car park, or may refuse to catch an alternative bus that uses a different routes even though it will reach the same destination. In each case, it is important to look at what the person with autism is able to do, not to undermine the strategies he has in place to enable him to do it.

Ruiz works as a trolley-collector at the local supermarket. His job is to collect the trolleys from around the car park and from the various trolley stations and to return them to the area in front of the building.

In order to do this, he has developed a routine where he walks clockwise around the first part of the car park, then collects from the first two stations and returns the trolleys to the building. He then starts at the second station, walks clockwise round the second part of the park and collects from the next two stations ... and so on. He has worked out this routine over a considerable period of time, and it is efficient. He knows, always, what he is doing and what he is going to do next. What is essential is that his supervisor does not suddenly demand that he empties the trolleys from the final station, or that he go to collect the trolleys near the entrance to the car park first. His supervisor needs to understand that Ruiz's reliance on routine is not limiting his ability to do the job well – far from it. It is allowing him to do the job at all, and producing a generally hard-working and efficient worker into the bargain.

Susan is a top student who is working at Doctorate level at university. She always arrives at the university a good hour before she is required to do anything. She finds the journey difficult and needs some quiet time on her own before she is able to function, and she has been given access to one of the staff study rooms in order to facilitate this. Similarly, she needs a similar period of preparation before she sets off on the journey home.

Clearly, there is nothing wrong with routines of these kinds as long as they are accepted and respected by those who work alongside the person with autism. Problems with routines do come, though, when they are based on wrong information.

For many people with autism the world is a highly confusing place, and sometimes the information used to make sense of it is not quite the right kind.

Sarah is being teased and persecuted by a group of girls at school. One day she gets up late and fails to have breakfast. That morning, quite by coincidence, the girls do not bother her. Sarah equates the 'empty' feeling in her stomach with the fact that she is not bullied. She finds, in addition, that if she avoids the lunch hall she is less likely to come to their notice. Sarah soon develops a whole routine around being hungry that 'keeps her safe', and is well on the way to developing an eating disorder.

Sameness and routine can be a huge help to a person with autism, as long as the information they are based upon is accurate. For the person who struggles to leave the house, a written list by the front door ("Have you switched off the oven? Do you have your keys? Do you have your mobile phone?) can be a tremendous help, and in time this written list may become internalised. For the person who is anxious about catching the bus, keeping the routine simple and repeatable ("Wait at the bus stop at the end of the road. Only get onto a number 4b. Have your bus-pass ready in your hand. Press the 'stop request' button as you pass the Post Office") can be a way to enable freedom, not restrict it. However, if a person with autism appears to be weaving routines that seem to make little sense, they may be worth some gentle investigation. It may be that they are perfectly valid, but it may also be that they are becoming like the worst kinds of superstitions – things that restrict your liberty and happiness and provide you with no actual protection whatsoever.

Anxiety and depression
A great many of the behaviours which we may see in a person with autism are, in fact, not symptoms of autism at all but are symptoms of anxiety and/or depression. Neither anxiety nor depression are intrinsic elements of Autism Spectrum Disorder, but it is a sad fact that for a great many people with autism, the struggle to live in the neuro-typical world brings with it both anxiety and depression. The world can be an alarming, a frightening, a lonely and a difficult place for the person with autism, and it is hardly surprising if anxiety and depression are the result.

It is important, though, to be very clear that neither anxiety nor depression are inevitable, and as such the presence of these conditions must be addressed, just as they would need to be in a non-autistic person. They have a cause – and as such they have a solution, and no person with autism should have to accept being frightened or unhappy, just because of the fact of their autism.

Anxiety in the person with autism is completely understandable. The person with autism lives in a world that is frequently unpredictable, and that is peopled by individuals who quite often make no sense at all. It is a world of light, colour, smell, sound, taste and touch which may, at any time, be overwhelming. It is a world where it is difficult, and sometimes impossible, to communicate wishes, desires, fears or uncertainties, and where it may be impossible to get clarification for what is not understood. It is a world that inspires anxiety, and anxiety is a natural response to it.

We all of us need to make sense of our environment if we are to feel safe in it. It is easy enough to imagine ourselves into situations where this security is taken away from us. Any situation where we lose our immediate and intuitive understanding of the people around us is likely to provoke anxiety.

Imagine being on a train in a country where you cannot speak the language. Suddenly a piercing alarm goes off. You do not know what this means – so you are frightened. You look to the people around you. All are waving small white tickets. You do not have a white ticket, only a green one – so you feel anxious. Next, some begin to embrace one another, some to bow and others to shake hands. You have no idea why – and you are alarmed that you will be expected to join in. Finally a guard comes along and shouts furiously at you, gesturing towards the roof of the train. You have no idea what you have done wrong or what is required of you. Others join in. You feel threatened, frustrated and stupid. You are suffering from anxiety.

In order to manage this strange environment again you make plans and you try your best to make sense of the world around you. You get into the habit of repeating what worked last time. You manage to make your journey by train successfully, with no alarming incidents, when you manage to sit on the single seat at the front .You decide to always try to get that seat from now on, and since yours is the first stop you succeed for many weeks. All seems well. Then, one day, you go to board the train and realise that all the seats have been removed and everyone is sitting on the floor, leaning back-to-back. You panic. Should you get on board? How will you know who to lean against? How does this work? What if you get it wrong?

Living in this world, as you can imagine, is extremely tiring. Even the most common-place activities, such as catching a train, take tremendous effort of thought and preparation. Even with the most careful planning, things still keep going wrong. There is no-one to turn to. You are alone, any help you are offered is inconsistent and often not what you wanted in the first place. Worst of all, you know that it is you who are different. Unlike the traveller in the strange land, you do not have your own country to which you can return. You do not have a 'people'. Even those who are described as having the same condition as you seem to be nothing like you. Is it surprising that you get depressed? Clearly, these are neuro-typical interpretations of what the world may be like for the person with autism. However, in my time talking to and just being with a whole variety of people with autism, both adults and children, I think they may be fairly accurate. So how can we help?

How can I help my brother to be less nervous and more confident?

What your brother, like our person on a train, needs more than anything else is accurate and reliable information. One of the accepted traits of a person with autism is often a need for facts. Factual information makes sense and, therefore, gives empowerment.

Our person on the train needs to know what the siren means – and he needs to know this information before the siren goes off so that he can predict it and not be alarmed by it. He needs clear information about what tickets are needed for travel. He needs information about correct protocol about how to behave around the other people on the train. He needs a clear 'fall-back' technique so that when he reached a situation that he couldn't predict (the anger of the guard) he had, for example, a card he could present that explained that he couldn't understand the language and that had further information on it – information about how the guard should respond, perhaps, or information about how to contact an interpreter. Finally, this information needs to be updated so that it remains relevant. The change in seating needed to be anticipated before it happened, and new information given about how to manage the situation.

Anxiety and depression can both be helped if the individual is empowered, if he is given more control over his own life and situation and is able to feel more confident about who he is, autism and all. No-one can – perhaps no-one should – cure the autism; however, we should all of us be working together to help cure and prevent the anxiety and depression.

Anger

Another characteristic in some people with autism, and one that concerns carers, other family members and indeed the wider community, is anger. Uncontrolled anger is alarming. The person with autism may lash out and may be intimidating. He may shout, hit out at others, at a wall, the floor, at himself. He may go into 'melt-down', where his behaviour goes out of control and physical restraint appears the only solution.

Concern about anger is understandable. However, as with anxiety and depression, anger is not an inevitable part of having autism, nor is it necessarily a problem.

There is nothing wrong with getting angry. It is an emotional response to a situation perceived by the individual as unjust, and as such is an entirely valid emotion. The point is that, although we all have a right to feel anger, we do not all have a right to express that anger by hitting out, breaking a person's window or spitting in their face. How we *express* our anger is far more likely to be a problem than the anger itself. Concern around a person with autism's anger is unlikely to be because of what the anger is about. It is far more likely to be about how that anger is expressed. Similarly, what is seen as 'anger' in many people with autism is in fact not anger at all. It may be frustration. It may be fear. It may simply be a learned behaviour which brings a predictable result. 'Anger', as a matter of concern around people with autism is far more likely to be to do with communication than with uncontrolled emotion.

Eli is ten. He is very happy playing on the computer but when the computer is turned off he used to shout, hit out at the person turning it off and sometimes throw himself on the floor and scream and kick. Much of this anger was recognised by his father as frustration at having no control over his world. He introduced a formal choice system where Eli could choose between turning off straight away and moving to a preferred activity, or instead staying on for a further set length of set time. He helped by making the choices 'easy'. For example, "You can turn off now and you have ice-cream and an apple or turn off in five minutes and have just the ice cream". In this situation Eli 'chooses' to give up the apple, 'chooses' to stay on the computer BUT 'chooses' to turn off after five minutes AND gets ice cream.

This is better than a straightforward reward system as it gives some power to Eli to control his own decisions, and it gives an agreed system for negotiating in the future.

Ray is a non-verbal fourteen-year-old who attends a residential school for young people with learning difficulties. There are various issues around his outbursts of 'anger' which he displays in quite specific situations, notably when taken to the shopping centre, when baked beans are put on his plate or when another child touches his Pokemon collection.

In each case, an angry outburst is the only way he has to express his feelings. The shopping centre is noisy and confusing with a whole unpredictable range of sights, smells and moving crowds; the baked bean juice soaks into his potatoes, the two tastes and textures together being utterly repellent to him (even though pleasant separately – like caviar and custard: perfectly nice if not taken together!) and his Pokemon collection is his current special interest, with many hours of his time spent ordering and organising it .In none of these examples is the emotion the problem, just the expression of the emotion. He needs support around managing the shopping centre environment but in the meantime, having another way to express himself (for example a 'No' card) might well reduce the need for an outburst. Understanding and respecting his wishes would go a long way to making his outbursts unnecessary. After all, providing a separate bowl for baked beans is probably a perfectly reasonable adjustment, and wanting a private personal space where possessions can be left safely is completely understandable for any fourteen-year-old.

In Ray's case, 'anger' is almost certainly both inability to communicate and the fact that the communication he does make is not listened to. If his anger outbursts are to be reduced, he has to be supported in having a different way to express fear or dislike, AND THIS EXRESSION HAS TO BE TAKEN SERIOUSLY. It is not much good expecting Ray to use a 'No' card if when he uses it he is taken to the supermarket anyway. He will quickly learn, especially as he gets bigger and stronger, that the 'No' card doesn't work where thumping his carer, lying on the floor and screaming are actually quite effective!

If there is a problem with communication it is always very important to try to work out what 'anger' is actually about. It may be fear, it may be frustration, it may even be pain. Someone who is non-verbal who has an ear infection may well appear to be 'angry'. He may be lashing out, biting, shouting and crying or banging his head in the floor. On the whole, rather than seeking to stop the behaviour, carers would do well to use the behaviour as communication, while working to find a 'better' (i.e. more socially acceptable) way to make that communication.

How can I help my son to avoid getting so angry?

I have already mentioned 'No' cards for someone who is non-verbal or who finds communication difficult, especially when under stress. In fact for many people with autism, effective communication may be the first thing to be lost when frightened, frustrated or overwhelmed. Some sort of simple device to express distress can help hugely to replace angry outbursts. This may be an 'Angry card' (a card that can be presented to a parent or teacher as an alternative to lashing out, but that is always taken seriously and the situation resolved) or an 'Exit card' (a card that allows the owner to escape from a situation to somewhere quieter in order to calm down before becoming overwhelmed). It may be a 'Frustrations book', something along the lines of a 'Case for the Prosecution', where someone with autism who has strong language skills can articulate the reasons for his anger, and come up with suggested ways to solve whatever the problem is.

What is important for the person with autism is to separate the emotion from the cause. Researchers at Cambridge University [The Journal 'Brain', 2009/BBC news 14/12/2009] have found some evidence that the brains of people with autism are less effective at processing information about themselves than those of neuro-typical people. People with autism may not understand or recognise their own thoughts and feelings, so may not have an 'early warning system' when becoming frustrated, angry or afraid. Because of this, emotions may overwhelm them very suddenly, resulting in their 'unpredictable' and apparently disproportionate 'anger'.

If the person can be helped to use a very simple and accessible system, such as a card, as soon as the emotion is recognised, it may well be possible to escape from whatever is causing the emotion and allow the person to avoid being overwhelmed. Then, once the situation has calmed down, the underlying cause can be explored and the person with autism helped to find alternative strategies to deal with it.

Clumsiness
Often a person with autism may have a slightly 'odd' gait. He

may appear clumsy or just generally give an impression of not being confident physically. In recent years this has come to be recognised as part of the condition's sensory processing differences. Proprioception is the ability of the brain to work out where various parts of the body are in relation to each other through interpreting the messages sent to the brain from the joints and muscles, and this seems to be weakened in many people with autism. Just as the typical teenager goes through a phase of being 'gawky' and clumsy when his arms and legs seem to have outgrown his understanding of them, the person with autism seems to have this difficulty throughout life. In addition, his sense of balance may be rather poorer than usual, possibly through problems with the vestibular system that interprets messages from the inner ear about movement and balance. The result is someone who may seek lots of sensory feedback (for example by enjoying jumping on a trampoline or swinging on a swing) or indeed someone who avoids motion of this kind, finding it makes him feel sick. The study of how the body regulates the messages from its various systems was pioneered by Dr A Jean Ayres some forty years ago, and is frequently referred to as study of Sensory Integration.

Nathan often bumps into other children in the playground, and he enjoys spinning, often turning round and round for many minutes without appearing to become dizzy. He has considerable trouble sitting still for any length of time, and always stands, leans over the table and rocks back and forth when doing any writing or colouring.

Max is in his forties. He finds it difficult to keep his balance, especially when moving through an environment such as a shopping centre where other people can change direction suddenly. He is only able to cross the pedestrian bridge over the railway line if he can hold onto the handrail, and he finds going down steps particularly challenging.

Perhaps as part of this 'clumsiness', many people with autism have considerable difficulty with fine motor skills such as doing up zippers and tying laces. Many, many people with autism struggle with handwriting, and this often has a catastrophic effect on their education. We all of us are quick to make spot judgements about a person because of their handwriting, and someone who continues to print into adulthood (i.e. who cannot manage 'joined-up' writing) and who may, for example, only write on the right-hand side of the paper and struggle to keep letters straight or of a consistent size may well be taken less seriously than someone who 'writes like a grown-up'.

Fortunately, increase in computer use means that most of us don't have to rely on handwriting any more, and so this particular prejudice against people with autism is gradually being overcome. It remains a problem for many pupils in school, though, and allowing a child with autism to use a keyboard can be one of the simplest yet most effective ways of helping to manage school. Similarly, although the school 'rule' may be to not allow mobile phones to be used in class, allowing the pupil with autism to photograph the whiteboard and then to listen, rather than trying to take notes and listen at the same time, can be an effective solution. Paper copies of presentations and pre-review of lesson material should, ideally, be routine.

There remains an element of clumsiness (or of an inability to 'read' the body's messages) that is seldom discussed in relation to having autism, yet which causes untold misery. Many children with autism are 'slow to get out of nappies', and indeed may continue to be incontinent into their teens or indeed into adulthood or for the whole of their lives. It seems that for some people with autism they may literally be unable to 'read' the internal signs that they need to empty bowels or bladder, and may be unaware that they have done so by accident until it is pointed out. Because autism is a hidden condition it may be difficult for many people to understand that a teenager who can quote the whole Periodic Table without a mistake may still not be reliable in using a lavatory, or that a happily employed father-or-two may nevertheless need incontinence pads.

The effect of this on an individual's acceptance by his peer-group, particularly perhaps through the secondary school years, can only too clearly be imagined. It may be necessary to fight vociferously on behalf of a person with autism in order to make sure that this aspect of the disability is understood and accepted and the person's self-image is not damaged irreparably.

What else?

There is more to having autism than using language in an unusual way, avoiding eye contact, having particularly strong interests and preferring sameness and routine. There is more than being angry or anxious or depressed, and certainly more than a clumsy gait or trouble interpreting the body's signals. So what is the 'more'? What might you expect from the child in your class with autism or from a work colleague who self-identifies as having Asperger syndrome?

Clearly, some elements of each of the above are likely, and an understanding of *why* certain characteristics or behaviours may be present, as described in part one, may well be a help too. In addition there are, of course, other bits and pieces.

It may well be, for example, that a person with autism may have unusual sleep patterns, perhaps needing very little sleep at all or finding it difficult to fall asleep. Curiously, this may be the single characteristic that many parents find most trying. Many people find that they cannot really 'switch off' as a parent until their children are safely asleep, and the fact that a child with autism seldom is, or seldom stays so, can be utterly exhausting. Many adults with autism find that 'swapping round', working at night and sleeping through the day, solves many of the social problems of having autism. Everything is quieter at night, there are fewer people and fewer pressures. Unfortunately, there may also be more dangers and care should be taken that a love for solitude and places away from the crowd does not lead a person with autism to being vulnerable. It is also true that there will be less opportunity for social interaction if the person is active at night, and this in itself can exacerbate social isolation. Some people with autism find it difficult to recognise the symptoms of tiredness in themselves, and for them a secure routine around 'bed time' may help. Certainly, for the child with autism a set and reliable bedtime routine can be essential (... for the parents' sanity, as well as for the child!)

Becoming nocturnal may exacerbate the problem that a person with autism may have little concept of danger. He may struggle to link cause and effect so that, for example, he steps out into the road without looking however many times he is reminded to wait and may, in addition, have a greatly reduced awareness of danger from other people. He may be naïve and believe that someone is being 'kind' if they tell him that they are, even if their intentions are malicious. Because of a reduced ability to read others socially, and because he may himself, unintentionally, be giving out 'wrong' signals, a situation may not be safe for an adult with autism even where it might be so for a neuro-typical person. Issues around relationships and sexual vulnerability need to be very carefully managed in order to make sure that a person with autism is helped to be safe.

One of the signs of autism in a child may be that he plays 'oddly' with toys, not using them as the manufacturer intended but lining them up, stacking them, spinning them or grouping them. His play may seem incomprehensible, although it will in fact have meaning to him. An adult with autism may 'act strangely', but only because his actions are not immediately interpretable by the neuro-typical public. One of the first steps to understanding a person with autism is to move from "What he is doing does not make sense" to "What he is doing does not make sense to me (...yet), *but I accept that it does to him!*"

Russell, 7, was repeatedly running at the wall, banging into it and spinning off. His mother watching him was seriously concerned and spent some time discussing his behaviour with his teacher. Was he distressed? Was he self-harming? Was this aggression or a sign of frustration? What had been happening at school to spark the behaviour? When Russell came across to join them his mother, rather tentatively, asked him what he had been doing. To Russell it was obvious. "I was being a beam of red light. All the other colours are absorbed into that wall, but, because it is painted red, I bounce off." No one could have guessed it, but there was perfect logic (and scientific accuracy!) in Russell's behaviour.

Having autism is to have a brain that works differently from that of the rest of the population. Because of this different working, there may be a number of different behaviours seen in the person with autism — but it is not the behaviours which make the autism, it is the different working of the brain. A person with autism may 'present' in any number of ways, and it is important that he (or she) is taken as an individual first rather than as a diagnosis. It is no good saying that "people with autism have trouble making eye-contact" if the person who has just come to work on your team makes eye-contact perfectly happily. The eye-contact is not the point; the autism is, and the only person who knows how that autism affects that individual is that individual him or herself. Yes, it is a good thing for the wider population to have some idea about 'what autism looks like', but it is not for us to pre-judge, and disbelief in a diagnosis does no-one any good at all. There are (many) ways that we can help to make the world a more welcoming place for the person with autism, as will be described in the next section. However, the most important is our willingness to accept and to try. A willingness in the rest of the population to take the time to see things from the person with autism's point of view would go a very long way to making the world make more sense to us all!

****

Chapter Three

What Can We Do To Help?

If we accept that people with autism are going to be part of all of our lives, and if we accept that there is much that our understanding of autism can do to make life better for these people, then what are these things? How can we help? If we believe our child has autism, if we are told that our colleague at work has Asperger syndrome, if we know that a student who is going to be in our tutor group at college has a diagnosis of ASD, then what?

There is no 'cure' for autism. Nothing we do is going to make the autism itself go away (and many people with autism would not wish it to go away anyway). However, if we understand what the issues are for the person who has autism, then we are in a much better position to understand the situation from their point of view. When they tell us that they need to get to the meeting an hour early, when they choose to miss events in the lecture theatre, when they go on and on about Japanese computer games or want their apple crumble and custard in separate dishes, our understanding of autism and our acceptance of it is going to make things so much easier for everyone.

But what more than that? What can we do pro-actively to help? How can we help to avoid all the damage to self esteem, the anxiety and the misery experienced by some people with autism and how can we help the person with autism to be confident and happy, secure about him or her self, autism and all?

This section looks at ways we can help. How much we choose to do so will depend, of course, on what the person with autism is to us. We are likely to do more and invest more time and effort on our child, or perhaps on our girlfriend, boyfriend or spouse, than we will on someone we meet once a month at the pub quiz. However, the same applies. If we know what we can do, at least we have the choice.

Getting a diagnosis

The first, and arguably the most important step in helping a person with autism, is to encourage that person to get a reliable diagnosis. Some people, perhaps particularly parents, can find this difficult. It can feel like 'labelling' your child, and the process of seeking a diagnosis can feel as if you are saying that there is 'something wrong' with him or her, which can feel like rejection. It can be painful to focus on apparent impairments in someone you love, and it can feel as if, by pointing them out, you are making them real where other people might not notice them. You don't want to have someone you love misdiagnosed and labelled as having a disability when they do not.

In fact, it can be reassuring that the diagnostic process is clinically specific and is becoming even more so. As long as you are able to get the person properly assessed then the diagnosis should be exact and accurate. It will, ideally, be carried out by an experienced, qualified, multi-disciplinary team and it is highly unlikely, in this case, that they will get it wrong. They will also be able to test to rule out other causes for concern, such as chromosome abnormalities or Fragile X syndrome. More mundanely, they will be able to make sure that your child doesn't fail to look at you because of eye-sight problems, or fail to respond to your voice because of deafness.

Finally, a full assessment is likely to include formal speech and language assessment and an assessment of intellectual ability. It can be a roller-coaster ride if, at the same time as being told that your child has autism you are told he has a top-of-the-range IQ or has elements of language-use several years beyond his age! Nothing is ever simple in autism, and even the most serious diagnosis will bring with it ways you can help. Perhaps that is the most important reason for diagnosis of all.

Getting access to that diagnosis is not always easy. The place to start is with your GP, ideally because your concerns have been listened to and therefore picked up by health visitors during the early months of your baby's life. Unfortunately this is not always the case.

Margaret was worried about her son's interaction with her almost from birth. He was a breast-fed baby, and since he was her second child with only fourteen months between his birth and that of his elder sister, Margaret remembered clearly how this 'should be'. When she expressed that she felt she could not connect with her baby to her health visitors, they consistently took her concerns to be signs of tiredness and post-natal depression, and insisted on treating her rather than assessing the baby. Because suggestion of post-natal depression was on her notes, she found it difficult to get her GP to take her concerns seriously later when she asked for a referral to a specialist.

When Marie finally plucked up the courage to go to her GP about her vague unease about her daughter's development, she was asked a barrage of questions – about the baby's sleep patterns, its feeding, its distress at being lifted, its being calmed by being wrapped in tight blankets – and when she was able to give examples of each of these was asked why she had not picked up on her daughter's condition sooner. She was left feeling that she, as mother, should have recognised the clinical presentation of a condition that doctors and health visitors had missed. As she commented, "If I had known my daughter was going to have autism, I would have read up about it in advance!"

The first point of call has to be the GP. If you are concerned, it may be advisable to write down your concerns, with examples, in order to present as clear as possible a case to your GP. Many GPs, perhaps because of financial pressures, are reluctant to refer on to specialists if they can help it. Some may even give an 'on the hoof' semi-diagnosis (such as "Presumed ASD" or "Autism-like presentation"), and if this is the case you need to be persistent. This is a serious diagnosis and you and your child have a right to have a full assessment by fully qualified specialists. There is no such thing as "A Touch of Autism" - either it is autism or it isn't, and you need to know which.

With persistence, you should be able to get your GP to refer on to a specialist. If you (or your GP!) are unsure of where or who a suitable specialist may be, the National Autistic Society Helpline **0808 800 4104** should be able to give you some names in your area.

There may, of course, be a considerable wait and this can be frustrating. You may be tempted to go privately and to pay for an assessment. This may help clarify matters for you, and help you in your own minds while you are waiting. However, it may be that a private diagnosis will not carry the same weight with schools, work-place, local authorities etc., so it is important to stay on waiting lists and still attend for full NHS assessment when it becomes available.

It can feel, while you are going through this stage, that getting the diagnosis is the most important thing in your life, especially if you are looking for a diagnosis in your child. Until you *know* if your child has autism, you cannot plan ahead and you may feel as if you cannot see what the future may hold. Getting the diagnosis, in this situation, can be a terrible let-down. Yes, it is a relief, to finally know for sure ... but where does that leave you?

Autism is such a wide-ranging, variably-presenting condition you still may be very unclear about just where that leaves him. Will he need care all his life? Will he need to go to a special school? Will he talk at all, and will what he says make sense? Will he be one of those people who is eccentric and odd but extrovert and confident, or someone who is frightened and anxious, a loner with no friends? None of these questions is likely to be fully answered by the diagnosis alone.

If the diagnosis is for an adult, then it may seem more like a key. Many adults choose to seek a diagnosis later in life just because they want to make sense of why they have always felt so 'different'. In this situation, finally having a full assessment, being taken seriously and understanding that the 'differentness' is because of a diagnosed condition can be a huge relief. At last, you might have an explanation for why so many things have been so difficult for so long. However, in each case, in child or adult, although a diagnosis explains *why*, it does not really make much clearer *what*.

What your child will be, just as what and who you are, is decided by life experiences, by upbringing, by luck and love and 'the roll of the dice'. A diagnosis is a hugely important, indeed an essential, place to start, but it is only that: the start.

Interacting with a person with autism

Once you are aware that someone has autism, you are in a much better position to change the way you interact with them. Communication is a two-way street, and if you have no diagnosed social impairment in this area, now is the time to put that to good use and adapt your way of interacting. A great deal of emphasis is placed, in many autism programmes, on guiding the person with autism to 'improve' their social interaction and communication skills. This puts all the pressure onto them; in fact, once the neuro-typical person has some understanding of autism, surely it is easier for that person to adapt and to make adjustment?

One of the most important advantages of your understanding, is that you are in a position to prevent misunderstanding. Often, a person with autism gets into difficulty because what he says or does is misunderstood or misinterpreted by those around him. He may be taken as rude or ignorant, as self-centred and boasting, as sly and untrustworthy, as aggressive or threatening, and each of these *is a mistake made by the neuro-typical person he is interacting with.* Perhaps the simplest way that we who are neuro-typical can help those who have autism is to try not to make so many mistakes!

Giles was in a school assembly at which the head teacher was talking about cutting back the trees and shrubs in her garden (the moral was about sometimes having to do negative things short-term in order for long-term growth). Unfortunately, about half-way into her presentation she mistakenly used the term cutting 'down' instead of 'back', with the result that her sentence was that she was "going to cut down her trees."

Giles had been sitting quietly, but at this he leapt to his feet in fury and began to lambaste his head teacher about how wrong it is to cut down trees ("they are the lungs of the planet" etc. etc.). There was a moment of stunned silence in the hall, which would normally (we can assume) be followed by Giles being removed from the hall, severely reprimanded, perhaps even suspended. However, his head teacher and indeed all the members of this small primary school knew Giles and were aware of his autism. They understood that this was an outburst of real, appalled passion and not an attempt to be 'naughty' or disrespectful. The head teacher reviewed her last sentence, recognised her error, corrected it and apologised for making it, and calm was restored instantly. Of course, there are few such schools (and certainly few such head teachers), but this remains an example of the very best of differentiation.

When interacting with someone with autism it is preferable to 'turn down' your own social sensitivity. When he walks away when you are in mid-sentence, fails to ask if you are feeling better when you have been off sick, tells you that you have new glasses (but not that they look nice) or goes to sit at another table at lunch, it is for you to remember not to take it personally. None of these is intended to have a sub-text and it would be wrong to read sub-texts into them. They don't indicate that you are boring or that you weren't missed, they don't suggest your glasses are ugly or that you are not worth talking to. Once you grasp this, you are far less likely to be hurt, even subconsciously, by what a person with autism does or says. Co-incidentally, the relief of not having to worry about watching out for a sub-text can be hugely refreshing. When you are with someone with autism you can forget office politics and the subtle battle for one-upmanship and get on with a more honest approach.

It may well be that you feel slightly nervous about how to interact with a person with autism. You may feel a sense of anxiety that you will get something wrong, a doubt that you will be able to 'read' the person and a worry that you will misunderstand or upset the person with autism. If you do, then hold onto that feeling! That feeling is how the person with autism probably feels most of the time. You cannot instinctively rely on your social awareness when dealing with this person; he cannot rely on it when dealing with anyone. Your feeling of discomfort is an excellent illustration for you of how the world must be for the autistic person, and because of your sophisticated theory of mind, you can use that experience to empathise with that person. Your skills, once again, can help to make the interaction so much more successful for you both.

Having established that you may need to adapt your usual reaction to the person with autism, it is a good idea to take a look at how you should adapt your approach to him too. This is likely to mean slowing down your speech and allowing processing time, not nervously filling silences with chatter but allowing time for the person to respond, respecting the person's private space and not approaching too suddenly or making physical contact without warning and generally trying to behave in as calm and predictable a manner as possible. Try not to bombard the person with questions and try not to make too many demands ("So, tell me all about yourself!"). Your language needs to be clear and unambiguous, avoiding metaphors and idioms. Above all, give yourself time to get to know this person, and for him or her or her to get to know you. All that is needed to start with is respect, and a willingness to try. Many people with autism experience crippling loneliness and social isolation. Your willingness to try could be their first step away from this isolation.

"...But what about me?", I hear you cry! You may be a kind and altruistic person, but is this going to be just a one-way street? We each of us want something back from the emotional investments we make. Why should you bother about this person if this person is not going to bother about you?

Why indeed – if this were the case. The person with autism is not a sponge, to take and give nothing back. A relationship requires input on both sides, whether in a loving marriage or an efficient work partnership. Just because a person with autism may struggle with social interaction and communication does not mean that there is no point in working to make a social connection. In spite of popular misconception and ignorance, autistic people *can* love, *can* be good and abiding friends, *can* be partners and parents. Many of the epithets for 'autistic' – loyal, trustworthy, straightforward, honest – describe the most desirable characteristics, whether in friend or work colleague, spouse or sibling. People with autism can, as well, be fascinating, funny, original, talented, inspirational and unforgettable, the same as any number of people without autism. It is important, always, to look beyond the 'deficit' to the person that it might be hiding.

Visual supports

Some people can get very hung up on the whole business of visual supports. Whole training programmes are offered on them, which are probably very useful and can come up with some really effective ways of offering support, but they are not strictly speaking necessary to get you started. So what actually, is a 'visual support'?

The idea behind this is that when you say something, it then disappears. I can say "My mobile number is 00446707863925", but most people are unlikely to be able to give me a call unless I help them out more than that. I might hand them a card with my number on it, write it down on a piece of paper or text my number through to them. Then that person will have an actual, visual record of the number that they can refer back to when they need to use it.

The person who has autism is the same, only may need this sort of visual prompt over rather more situations. When told something, his brain is likely to process the information rather differently to the way a neuro-typical brain does, and it can all take rather longer. Perhaps he is struggling to manage a metaphor or recall a requested detail. The result can often be that much of what else is said is lost.

Owen's teacher asked the class get their homework diaries out. She then said, "Remember how we were looking at the effects of de-forestation on the rainforests? I want you to design a poster to encourage pupils at this school to be more careful about re-cycling." Owen followed the first of these instructions and placed his diary on the desk. He then thought back and could indeed remember the details explored in the lesson about deforestation. However, as he was doing this he failed to take in the information about the work, or even to realise that homework was being set. He certainly didn't think to write it in the diary, since he was never instructed to do so. The chances of Owen being able to complete the homework successfully are rather slim.

A 'visual support' in this incidence would have been invaluable. Ideally, this would have been a sheet with the instructions for the homework assignment detailed in clear, unambiguous steps. This would have given an opportunity for many other of the imponderables of the task to be made clearer. What size poster? Should it be in colour? Can it be created on the computer? Should it deal with all recycling or just concentrate on materials used by the students? How long should Owen take on the task? When should the poster be handed in, where and to whom? Even if this were not possible, at very least Owen would have been helped if "Design a poster to encourage recycling in school" had been written by the teacher into Owen's homework diary.

A visual support can be anything that can be looked at to provide reference. It can range from a Post-it note stuck on the front door saying "Collect parcel" through a large "Dentist!" penned in red on the calendar to a visual step-by-step guide to how to assemble a wardrobe. We most of us use visual supports all of the time. The trick is to remember how helpful they can be for the person with autism.

Glen is eight .Every morning he gets out of bed and sees his Morning Chart on his wall. The first item on this is a picture of the bathroom. Once he is in the bathroom there is a picture of the toilet, then of the handbasin, then of a toothbrush. Glen is now able to use each of these without further prompts, but to get to that stage, each was itself broken down into small visual steps. Brushing his teeth used to mean following a picture chart showing the toothbrush, then the toothpaste, then the toothpaste being squeezed onto the brush, then an open mouth ... and so on. Glen no longer needs these visual supports, and the reminder to brush his teeth is sufficient. When he gets back to his room he lifts the picture of the bathroom off the chart and puts it into a 'Finished' box. He then moves to the next item, which shows clothing. He can now get dressed into the clothes that his mother has laid ready without further prompting, but to get to that point he went through using pictures for each item. Glen's gradual and growing independence has come through consistent use of visual support that breaks down the tasks of his life into manageable sections.

Max is thirty-eight and works full time in a responsible position in an office. His colleagues all understand that he prefers instructions, notices, plans and comments to be emailed to him, or for them requested via the on-line calendar. Max cannot manage if a colleague casually suggests a change of plan while they are both, for example, at the coffee machine or having lunch. Max keeps his online diary highly detailed and accurate for each day, week and month, and as long as all items are entered into this Max works extremely well. He is known by his colleagues as meticulous and a little inflexible, but also as utterly reliable.

One of the more useful visual supports for many people with autism is a schedule. This tells the person what to do, and what will happen next. If, for example, it is a schedule of the school day it gives pictures or words to explain that morning assembly will be followed by circle time, then by P.E., playtime outside and an art activity. The great thing about a schedule like this is that changes can be flagged up visually. If it starts to rain, the symbol for Outside Play can be replaced by one for Wet Indoor Play. For the young child with autism who struggles to manage change and unpredictability, understanding what is happening can be hugely reassuring. In the same way, texting through to a teenager that there has been a change of room for a lecture or 'flagging up' with an email that there is going to be a routine fire alarm at work can save a great deal of unnecessary distress.

Richard lives in a residential care home for adults with autism and additional learning difficulties .Richard used to become extremely upset and agitated whenever a new or different carer came on duty. The staff have overcome this by having a 'duty board' for the day with photographs of the carers on duty that day. If there is someone new expected, his photo is taken and added to the board before he starts work. Photographs of all the carers who work at the home but who are off-duty are displayed on a different board. In this way Richard can see at any one time who is at the home and who is not there that day but is still part of the team, which has greatly reduced his distress.

Sometimes a visual support can be as simple as colour-coding, as in colouring the school timetable and different curriculum subjects. Other times a notice or sign can be a quick and efficient way to communicate, as seen all around us in Emergency Exit signs, road signs and the like. Many of these can be adapted to help a person with autism. The classic 'not allowed' sign of a red circle with a diagonal red line, familiar to us all (think of the 'No

Smoking' sign) can be adapted to mean 'No Hitting', 'No chewing your sleeve' or whatever, and can be a powerful tool. Visual support can be given around time management and when an activity will change. A visual countdown dial to show when a session on the computer will end is likely to reduce the problems for a person with autism. A map of an unfamiliar building, a seating plan to show where to sit, a photograph of a holiday house — each are visual ways of helping to make things clearer and less threatening for a person with autism.

The great thing about a visual support is that it stays there and it stays consistent. A check-list by the front door ("Shoes? Coat? Keys? Bus pass? Money?") may well be so much more efficient (as well as so much less infuriating all round!) than just verbally asking a person with autism to get ready to go out.

Accepting all communication
Because a person with autism will have a diagnosed impairment in social communication, it is important that every effort is made by the rest of us to help communication occur. I have already discussed how we can try to work harder at not misunderstanding the person with autism, at not misinterpreting gaze direction or seemingly unfriendly comments. As well as not misunderstanding, it is important that we work at accepting all communication as it is offered.

Luke is a non-verbal four-year-old with a diagnosis of autism. There are two routes from his home into town, one which involves crossing a low foot-bridge over a stream and one which uses a much bigger road bridge. Luke is perfectly happy to cross the road bridge, but if taken to the foot bridge would cry, scream, cover his ears and curl up on the floor.

His parents are not sure what it is about the bridge that frightens him. He is still small enough that if they wish they could ignore his protests and simply pick him up and carry him over the bridge. However, what they chose instead was to accept his reaction as communication.

His mother varied the route into town. If they went the foot-bridge way she waited for Luke's first sign of objection and promptly stopped. She squatted down to his height and asked him, "No?". She waited and gave Luke every opportunity to respond. As soon as he gave even so much as a grunt or a sound, she turned round and went the other way. In a matter of days Luke was echoing with "Nuh" and now says "No" independently as soon as they approach the bridge .He no longer cries or screams, and his mother ALWAYS turns round and goes the other way. Luke has found that his communication of the word "No" works very well. His parents are building on this, giving him 'choices', such as a breadstick or a piece of chocolate. They offer him the breadstick and encourage him to say "No" before giving the chocolate. The next step, they hope, is for him to say "Yes" for what he does want, and ultimately to name it and to continue to expand his vocabulary. This emerging speech has all come out of accepting his behaviour regarding the bridge as communication.

The example above has taken considerable patience and respect from Luke's parents. Sadly, many people would have seen his behaviour as 'autistic' and as something that had to be put up with in a non-verbal child. For some, the attitude would have been, "He shouts and screams because he is autistic", with no reference to either why, or what it meant. Luke's parents had the understanding to change a difficult situation into an opportunity for communication. Their reward for accepting his communication of fear *as* communication is immense. Luke is, after all, no longer truly 'non-verbal'.

In Luke's case it was necessary to accept crying, shouting and distressed behaviour as a way to communicate. If his parents had been concentrating only on stopping the 'autistic behaviour' and not seen beyond this to a chance to interact, they would have missed a golden opportunity. Often the focus with a person with autism will be on stopping or altering behaviour, and the essential communication element of that behaviour will be missed.

Luke's parents could have stopped the shouting and screaming. In earlier, more barbaric times it was considered acceptable to 'teach' an autistic child not to do something through aversion association. If when Luke started to scream he had had water squirted in his face, for example, he might well have learned not to scream. Even if such methods are no longer acceptable, Luke's parents could quite easily have used the most common one: they could have ignored Luke's behaviour. In the end it is likely that Luke would have given up. He may well have continued to be just as frightened or upset by the bridge, but in the end he may have ceased even trying to indicate this. After all, what would be the point?

Luke's parents took the completely opposite approach. They never demonised the shouting and crying, but instead accepted it, even welcomed it as communication. However, what they did do was provide Luke with a much more effective way of communicating, by giving him the word "No". The incidental by-product of this was that the shouting and screaming ceased — not because Luke had given up and withdrawn but because he had been given a so much more effective communication tool.

This attitude can be expanded to embrace all sorts of situations involving people with autism. As soon as the neuro-typical person gets away from a focus on altering behaviour, and moves instead to a focus on accepting behaviour as communication, all sorts of problems can be sorted out.

Toby was repeatedly in trouble for spitting at other children at school. His teacher and support assistant had tried many ways to stop him, from reprimanding the behaviour and applying sanctions to running a reward chart for days without an incident. Toby continued to spit. Toby's language level was good, and the staff were confident that he understood what they wanted.

It was only when they took the spitting as communication that they made any progress. Toby's spitting was a way of making other children move away from him. It meant, in fact, "I want more space." As soon as this was understood, Toby was given a phrase to use instead ("Please would you not stand so close to me") and was also allowed differentiation such as being allowed to step out of the line of children waiting to go in at the end of break, and to keep his coat and shoes in the classroom to avoid having to use the overcrowded cloakroom. This was very effective, and Toby stopped spitting within a week.

Raymond was causing increasing frustration to his support worker because he would never ring the office when he was supposed to. The support officer took considerable trouble making sure that the times were suitable to Raymond and always double-checked all arrangements. Still Raymond would fail to ring. The support officer took the failure to ring as communication that Raymond did not want to use the telephone. They rearranged their contact to take place by text and Raymond became punctual and reliable.

A person with autism has, by definition, a difficulty with social communication. His communication methods may appear clumsy, or may be misunderstood as rude or defiant. By stopping and asking the question, "What is he trying to tell me?", the neuro-typical person can do so much not only to help the communication but to help the person with autism to learn to communicate more effectively. Even when it is difficult, communication is almost always the most important goal.

Keeping him safe

One of the things that becomes apparent as you become more aware of a person with autism is just how frighteningly vulnerable he or she may be. Naivety, an inability to 'read' a social situation, clumsy language use that can cause offence or be taken to be aggressive or predatory, misinterpretation of other people's actions – all are examples of ways that a person with autism can run into difficulty or even danger.

One of the most important reasons for getting a diagnosis for a child is because it should afford him some protection at school. Without a diagnosis it is quite likely that his behaviour will be interpreted as defiant or 'naughty', and he may find himself in trouble without any idea of the reason.

Liam was four and had just started Nursery. His teacher reported that he "refused" to sit quietly with the other children at milk time, and that she had to sit him on the 'Thinking Chair' by himself day after day. Liam was also "very naughty" when it came to coming in from playtime, taking no notice of the whistle and continuing to run up and down at the perimeter fence where he spent all of his time. She reported that he "didn't listen" at carpet time, frequently sitting facing in a different direction to the other children. Liam was diagnosed with autism just before his fifth birthday.

Matias was repeatedly in trouble at his new Middle school, even though his First school had reported him to be an able and compliant pupil. Particular 'triggers' for his apparent misbehaviour were both the science labs and art rooms, where he "wandered about", and his general slowness and lateness to most lessons. Matias was shadowed for a day by a student teacher, this trainee observed that rather than wandering about, Matias was doing a circuit of the labs and the art room, checking that all the taps were off. She also observed that he was late to lessons as before leaving any class he would go round switching off lights and closing doors (much to his teachers' annoyance, who described him as "irritating"). Matias's behaviour was initially diagnosed as Obsessive Compulsive Disorder, although later this was amended when he received a diagnosis of Asperger syndrome. The student teacher observed that the school used a number of stickers ("Please switch off lights before leaving the room", "Turn taps OFF", "Please shut the door"). These had been there for so long they were functionally invisible to most members of the school, but they were glaringly obvious to Matias. His attitude to his new school, reinforced daily by his mother, was that if he obeyed all instructions, he would do well.

Once a child has a diagnosis of an Autism Spectrum Disorder there is a much greater chance that his behaviour will be understood and not misinterpreted as difficult or confrontational. Of course, this presupposes a good understanding of autism in teachers and support workers. Such understanding is growing slowly, but it may be that an autism professional (or a parent) will still need to interpret for the autistic pupil. Nor does a pupil in school need only to be kept safe from being misunderstood by adults. Much of the 'danger' of school comes from the other pupils. Pupils with autism are particularly vulnerable to bullying, and considerable work needs to be done to ensure that they are able to be safe in school.

Sadly, children are not the only ones vulnerable to bullying. If an adult with autism manages to secure a job, he or she will still have to deal with the social context of that job. Being ostracised and left out, being made the butt of jokes, not being granted working conditions that make allowances for autism needs, being passed over for promotion or being unfairly dismissed may all still occur in the adult world. Having said that, disability rights are gradually becoming more powerful, and a diagnosis of autism does bring with it some protection. Accessing this can be daunting, and often what a parent or supporter can most usefully do is to help the person with autism to negotiate the system.

Helping someone with autism to be safe can be as much as explaining the diagnosis to a teacher or supporting an adult to access disability rights, or it can be far more simple. If you are with someone with autism you can often 'head off trouble' before it has a chance to take hold. Often a quiet piece of advice ("Don't stare at her", "You should talk about something other than wind turbines now", "Stop humming") can go a tremendous way towards helping a person with autism. Simple advice such as keeping to a lit path home, not starting conversations with people on the underground, walking away if starting to get angry or not wearing your 'Away Supporters' football scarf on the train home can all make a difference. We are conditioned not to interfere, and seldom feel that we can (or should) give advice to adults, even if we know that what they are doing may put them into danger. If you are aware that a friend or colleague has autism, talk to him and find out whether he thinks this should be the case with him. It may well be that all he needs to achieve increased independence is someone who will give him advice like this when he is set to go wrong, and who will be someone he can ask when he has a question about what is the best way to behave. Social isolation means not having people to turn to in this way, yet the person with autism is more likely, not less, to need continued guidance into adulthood. There is an old saying that there are some things only your best friend will tell you, specifically about personal appearance and personal hygiene. If someone with autism smells, you are not being a friend if you feel it would be 'rude' to mention it. Tell him the problem, quite simply and without embarrassment. Advise showering daily, cleaning teeth, changing clothes or whatever. If you do so in a straightforward, non-judgemental way merely stating the facts, you should avoid hurting the person, and the positive results for him and his social acceptance can be huge.

Most people learn to be safe – to avoid danger, argument, ridicule and rejection – through talking to and observing friends. Hours of teen-life are spent working out what is and what is not acceptable, especially as regards behaviour towards the opposite sex. How to look, how to talk, what not to do, how to attract others and how to escape from unwanted attention, all are discussed and refined over hours and hours of social interaction. For the person with autism, these hours may quite simply be missing. Because he or she may well not have that social interaction experience through the years of growing up, that knowledge may never be acquired. Sadly, few who are going through adolescence themselves have the self-confidence to include someone who has social communication and interaction difficulties, and that person may well lack the social imagination skills to infer learning from observing those around. Perhaps one of the main things we can be, for the person with autism, is that missing 'friend'.

Encouraging friendships

So what is a friend? It may seem an odd question, but for the person with autism it is relevant. Most of us have a range of people who come under this rather loose descriptive title, ranging from someone who often comes along when our group goes out and whose name we know but little else about them right through to the person we would turn to first in trouble and whom we would trust to raise our children if we died. That is quite a range! For the child with autism one of the first problems may be difficulty making friends. What constitutes a friend changes depending on age and development. Professor Tony Attwood has written widely on understanding and assisting with the development of friendship skills in young people with autism, both in his books and on his website. He has broken-down and analysed the skills needed to develop friendship, and has provided a check list to use to define where friendship skills are lacking and need more support. What is certain is that a person with autism is likely to need support in order to develop friendships.

If the person we care about is our child, we can try to support the development of friendship by providing opportunity. We may have to be the ones to invite another child round to play, and we may need to be on hand to help the session run smoothly. Perhaps we can provide a structured activity whether this be helping the children to bake cakes or paying for trampoline sessions or a round of mini-golf. Perhaps we can encourage our child to join an organised group such as Cubs, and be on hand by being a parent-helper to support his involvement. Perhaps we can be the ones to be on the lookout for groups of people who share interests in common with our child, signing him up to the local sci-fi club or helping him to search on-line for a group who have the same passion for military aircraft. However, try though we might, facilitating the development of true friendship is never easy. The parties themselves have, both of them, to want to develop the relationship and have to have the skills to do so. For the child with autism this can remain a problem.

What we may end up doing for our child is what we certainly can offer to our work colleague or new acquaintance with autism: we can be that friend. It can be tremendously difficult to get other children or adolescents to adapt sufficiently that they are able to accept a young person with autism into their friendship group. We can try, but as adults we will never be able really to access the situation 'from the inside'. On the other hand, now that we are adults we are able to offer that level of adaptability and understanding that we lacked when we were younger. Now is the time that we are ideally placed to offer that missing friendship to the person with autism.

Even as adults we are often cautious about our friendships. Will being friendly with this person reflect badly on us with our colleagues? Will the person with autism be too demanding and expect to take up all of our time? Will we get the social reciprocity we crave from the situation or will it be a one-way street? Do we, indeed, have the skills to be able to form a friendship with someone we may not wholly understand?

Most of these questions can be answered by being very clear about what the friendship we are offering or seeking entails. We need to be clear in our own minds about what commitment of time and energy we are ready to offer. Perhaps we need to be clear about this to the person with autism too. Most friendships require clear boundaries. You may feel, with a new friend, that it is acceptable to text but not to telephone. You may be happy to meet for coffee but not to spend the whole day together. You may be happy to talk together for part of the evening but want to move on to talk to other members of the group later on. If you are clear about these boundaries you are more likely to be able to express them to a person with autism. If you are going to become friends with this person, being able to communicate your wishes, in a way that is understood, is going to be as important as learning to understand that person's wishes. How are you going to be sure whether that person finds your demands intrusive? How will you know when that person really would rather be left in peace? The communication 'ball' is likely to be in your court, since you are the one with the social skills. Now is the time to put those skills to good use!

Martin has recently been taken on as a member of staff at a department store. Laura is aware that he has autism, as her brother has the same diagnosis. She is keen to help Martin, is happy to help him to 'fit in' and enjoys spending time with him.

She knows enough about autism not to be offended when he comes into the staff room and goes to sit at a different table. She asks if she may join him or whether he would rather be on his own. When he says that she may join him they spend their break together. When the break is over she explains that she has arranged to meet other colleagues over lunchtime. She checks her break schedule against his, confirms that they will both be free at the same time on the following day and says that perhaps they may be able talk further then. She leaves after saying that she has enjoyed spending her break period with Martin and that she is glad that he has come to work at the store.

Laura is the one who is 'controlling' this developing friendship, but she is doing so in an open and easy-to-follow manner, and is trying her best to be sensitive to Martin's wishes. Martin is being given clear boundaries, is being given opportunities to request greater space and is being given clear messages that Laura is being friendly.

Friendships – relationships in general – are complicated, complex and often unfathomable things, even to those of us without autism. The precise nature of them, how they develop and what each party gives and gains is often hard to pin down. What is certain, though, is that they begin by one or other of the parties making the effort to cross the invisible boundary between 'stranger' and 'accepted'. One party in any friendship will have instigated that first move, when he or she signalled acceptance of the other person. For we who do not have autism often this initial acceptance of the person with autism, including the autism spectrum aspect of that person, can be the most important thing that we can offer. True and lasting friendship may take longer, but at least we can be the ones to reach out and give a helping hand over the initial hurdle.

Accepting the autism

Ultimately, so much of what we can 'do to help' the person with autism is about accepting the autism in them. When a parent first gets a diagnosis of autism, most will ask about a 'cure'. Most are likely to begin by seeing the autism as something additional to the person, something that (they wish) could be taken away, leaving their child free to be the person they had thought he was or had wanted him to be. The autism spectrum isn't like that. There isn't the person, and then the autism that is 'getting in the way'. Autism isn't a disease or an illness, and it can't be corrected like short-sightedness. When autism is described as a Pervasive Developmental Disorder that means that it pervades the whole being of that person, and affects their whole development. Who they are is the person with autism. If you took the autism away, they wouldn't be themselves any more.

I said earlier that it is important to "look beyond the 'deficit' to the person it might be hiding". This is not to imply that autism is a bolt-on, and that there is another person behind the barrier that it puts up. That would only be true if we view the autism as the deficit, rather than the problems that it throws up as that deficit. What we need to do is to see the autism, instead, as integral to the good in the person. The person with autism doesn't have to "be okay in spite of the autism"; he or she can "be okay including the autism". This accepting of autism is perhaps the greatest thing we can do for a person with ASD, especially if our acceptance can help that person accept the autism in him or her self. Yes, having an autism-spectrum difference means that that person has problems in certain social areas. However, if we can help that person to see that we accept them, that we don't 'mind' these areas of social difficulty and can either overlook them as unimportant or are happy to help to overcome them, then we can help the person with autism to be a lot happier about who they are.

What we are doing is saying, "You have autism. I understand what that means and I am not going to take offence at your ASD-prompted behaviour. I am happy to take a little extra time to make sure that we understand each other because you are worth it!"

Rachel has recently become engaged to Ethan, who has a diagnosis of autism. She loves and admires him, finds him wildly attractive and cannot believe how happy he has made her by suggesting they get married. She accepts that some of his behaviour socially is unusual and that sometimes he says things that she finds strange. She finds the insight that he gives her into a whole other way of viewing the world as fascinating and exhilarating. Both Rachel and Ethan are aware that his autism needs to be 'factored in' to the developing relationship (including, they hope one day, into that with their children), and both are active in exploring what it means for their ongoing interaction.

Oliver is a popular member of the crew on a cruise liner. Because of the nature of the job, the crew rely on each other socially over considerable periods of time, and Oliver has had – and continues to have – to work hard at understanding the complex social interactions of the group. He is open about his autism, and is happy to tell people that he is "the sort of person who sometimes misunderstands things." He has an agreement with the rest of the crew that when he is being boring about his special interest, they will tell him to stop and he takes this in good part. He has also agreed with them that if he thinks that someone is being rude or unpleasant, he will check with another crew member before taking offence. In return, the rest of the crew respect Oliver's need for consistency and routine and have accommodated his request to stick to a limited number of well-rehearsed duties. They all 'look out for him' and are ready to intervene if his social difficulties look like leading him into problems with one of the passengers.

Oliver's description of himself as "the sort of person who…" is interesting. Having autism can make you the "sort of person who needs a routine", or the "sort of person who prefers things written down." It can mean that you are the "sort of person who prefers to arrive early" or the "sort of person who cannot cope with certain strong smells." We most of us accept that there are different sorts of people in this world, and that all kinds of people have all kinds of needs. Accepting that a person with autism has these needs and is worth knowing anyway is perhaps the very best thing that any of us can do for that person.

****

Chapter Four

What About School and Work?

Realistically, to 'get on' in life most of us will need to manage the demands of school, and then of some kind of work. For the person with autism, each of these is a considerable challenge.

School is a highly social institution, where the ability to fit in counts strongly, and the penalties for failing to do so can be high. A child with autism may have a huge range of school experiences – from special school through to mainstream, from nursery through to higher education – but in each the academic demands are only one part of the challenge. Making sense of the environment and of the people in that environment can throw up particular issues for the autistic pupil. Similarly, although an adult with autism may be highly able, the social context of most work environments means that only a small percentage of adults with an autism diagnosis will manage to secure full-time work. Clearly, if a person with autism is to be supported to be independent, there is a great deal that needs to be done. But what?

This section looks at the ways that each of us, friends, parents, colleagues, teachers and employers of individuals with autism can help. It does not deal with the institutional approaches, neither how education could or should be improved for those with autism nor with Disability or Employment rights and law. Each of these is hugely important, but is dealt with elsewhere (the National Autistic Society website is a good place to start for information on these matters). What this section looks at is the help that we can give, all of us, 'on the ground', to those with autism in our communities.

Motivation

One of the first issues that are likely to strike anyone who has tried to teach a child with autism is that of motivation. The neuro-typical pupils sit there (at least at first!) eager to please, to catch your eye, to earn praise or a star on their chart and to make their parents proud. Yet for the pupil with autism, each of these may be utterly irrelevant. All of the usual motivators that teachers use such as displaying work on the wall, reading work aloud, signalling a pupil out for a round of applause or to be 'Star of the Week', these may simply not work with a pupil who has autism, since all of these motivators are socially constructed.

Rhys struggles to sit with the other children on the carpet at the beginning and end of each session. His teacher, keen to encourage him, watched carefully for that split second when Rhys was sitting quietly and correctly, and pounced with immediate praise and the award of a 'Good Work' sticker. From Rhys' point of view, as soon as he had sat down he was being told to stand up again, and was having a sticker put on his jumper. Since he has a strong aversion to stickers (disliking the glue and knowing that it attracts germs), this has made sure that he will avoid sitting on the carpet again at all costs.

So how could Rhys' teacher have encouraged Rhys to sit with the other children? How is she to motivate him to do what she wants, and how can she reward him when he does?

Rhys now has a blue carpet square, which is placed to the side of the group of children at carpet time. He knows that this is his place, so his teacher can now be sure that Rhys does know where to sit (his behaviour previously could as easily have been because of confusion as because of any wish not to comply). As long as Rhys is sitting quietly on the blue square he is allowed one of the construction toys that are his greatest interest to play with. In return, after a short time (indicated by a visual timer) has elapsed, he is free to move off to play in the quiet corner with the toys instead of sitting with the other children. This allows him to avoid the singing and clapping time, which his behaviour suggests he finds uncomfortable.

There are a number of factors to this strategy. First of all, the teacher has made sure that Rhys understands what is needed to do the activity 'correctly'. It would be unfair to penalise Rhys if he simply doesn't understand what is required of him (...and the instruction to "Come and sit on the carpet" is a strange one when the whole classroom is carpeted!). Now that she is sure that he knows what is required of him, she combines a reward with a distractor to help him to achieve the task.

For many people with autism, having something tactile to focus on and move around in the hands can be tremendously therapeutic. She has also accepted that the singing session at the end of the day, when Rhys is likely to be tired anyway, is more than he can cope with. The opportunity for Rhys to play quietly, rather than having to join in this session, is something that works for both of them.

So could this way of providing differentiation be adapted for an older pupil, or indeed for an adult in the workplace? After all, an older individual with autism is likely to be more able to articulate his needs so that less will be down to guess-work on behalf of the teacher. As long as those who work with an individual with autism are ready to willing and to adapt, surely it shouldn't be too difficult.

Grete works for a busy and vibrant magazine as a copy editor. She attends the twice-weekly meetings, but always arrives a minute or two 'late' after the rest are seated, and always sits in the same place, which is reserved for her. It is accepted that she often looks as if she is not listening as she seldom looks at the speakers and is often paying more attention to her mobile phone .Grete never attends the Friday mid-day meeting, which is an informal affair conducted over lunch. She receives a written report of the salient points, and then leaves early for the weekend. Every few weeks, when she feels she needs to, she takes several days to work from home. Her employers see no problem with this, or with any of the differentiation she has put in place to allow for her autism. Her work is of an extremely high standard. She is meticulously accurate and utterly reliable about deadlines. Their only disappointment is that she repeatedly resisted their attempts to promote her.

Grete is motivated by the job itself, which she enjoys doing. She does not see the need to alter that job by accepting promotion, especially as that would involve a management role and she has enough self-knowledge to understand that she would not find managing other people easy or rewarding. She has put into place a number of ways to help herself to manage her working environment, and her employers are astute enough to understand that these are well worth their while honouring.

In Grete's case the job itself is rewarding. Indeed, this can often be the case and we must be careful not to undervalue the satisfaction of a job well done to a person with autism. Where the neuro-typical person might become bored with sameness, or be more interested in forging and maintaining a variety of social relationships, a person with autism may get genuine satisfaction from achieving the day's tasks.

However, be aware that believing that a person with autism is achieving job satisfaction must never be an excuse for neglecting him, failing to offer social support or failing to support that person in promotion or job development if he wishes it.

Of course, some jobs, and some lessons at school, may never be attractive. Most of us get through Geography or Design Technology or through the holiday job stacking the supermarket shelves because we have to. Perhaps we switch off and go into a day dream. Perhaps we plan what we will spend our earnings on. Perhaps we get through in anticipation of whether we'll be asked out during the lunch break. In each case we have our coping strategy, and most of us will find something to help us get through our day.

The person with autism may be uniquely gifted in the way he can 'switch off'. Many people with autism have an intense and vivid inner world, and certainly many pupils with autism spend a great deal more of their time in that world than they do in the often hostile and confusing 'real' world of school! Motivating someone who has access to this dimension to come out and join this world can be a challenge, and sometimes, perhaps, to do so can be to miss the point. What can be a motivator, for many people with autism, is the opportunity to have some time alone, in that inner world. Having a quiet space and a quiet time in which to have the opportunity to recharge can be enough to allow many people with autism to manage environments such as school and work.

Of course, it is also important to realise that a person with autism is likely be motivated in his job, as are most people, by the money (and the fact that this allows him to add to the 1980s music magazine collection which is his passion) and by the feeling of self-worth and independence that employment gives. Where this is the case, what are the barriers to prevent him from achieving this goal?

Understanding the environment

Sometimes the barriers that prevent a person with autism from accessing school or work are physical ones. Often quite simple adaptation of the working or learning environment can make enormous differences.

Charlie is fourteen .He has his own desk in each of his mainstream classrooms, always by the window and never shared with another pupil. He is allowed to leave lessons five minutes before the bell, and to go into his next classroom as soon as it is available, before the other pupils. During individual work in any lesson he is permitted to wear earpieces and to listen to music or white noise. Charlie has permission not to wear the school uniform shirt and tie but instead wears the softer polo neck uniform designed for PE.

Charlie's environment is being adapted to meet his needs. He is allowed his own desk so that he knows where to sit in each classroom, and so that he has his own defined space and is not having to deal with intrusion by another person. He leaves class early to avoid the crush and jostle of the busy period between change of lessons, and is allowed into the classroom first in order to set up his environment – his lap-top, books, pens and pencils – before the lesson begins. His desk is by the window in each case to make the best use of natural light as he finds the pulsing of the overhead fluorescent bulbs distracting. He listens to music or white noise in order to shut out the rest of the class and allow him both to concentrate on the task and to have some 'own time' to repair. He found the tight feeling of shirt and tie around his neck very distressing, and the compromise of the polo shirt has meant that he is not having to struggle, throughout the day, with a feeling of claustrophobia and choking.

Each of these adaptations are to do with Charlie's physical environment. They do not address social communication or interaction differences, but deal solely with making Charlie's physical experience more acceptable to him. What they do achieve is to allow Charlie to cope much better with these aspects of his autism for himself.

When first starting in a school or work, some time spent assessing the physical challenges of the environment, and what can be done to overcome them, can make a tremendous difference to the successful outcome for the person with autism. Inclusion means finding a way to include that person, making adjustments to allow for their differences. It should be stressed that this is needed, even if it means treating the person with autism in some ways more favourably than their neuro-typical counterparts. Allowing Charlie to wear a different version of the school uniform does not undermine the uniform code of the school. The old argument, that other pupils will say, "If he wears that, why can't I?" really doesn't hold water. The answer, of course, is that the neuro-typical person cannot wear the polo shirt because he does not have autism. To argue against this is as ludicrous as an argument suggesting that it is unfair for a person who uses a wheelchair to be 'allowed' to sit down during the National Anthem. The reason is the disability, and the objections should quite simply stop there.

For Charlie's environment to have been adapted successfully, the institution (in this case the school) had to be ready to listen to his needs, to understand and to adapt. Given that Charlie has a diagnosed difficulty with social communication, this meant that the school had to make a positive effort to understand his needs, not merely wait until he articulated them. It is not good enough for a school or employer to say, when the pupil or employee leaves because of the stress of trying to manage the noise levels, the clothing requirements, the lunchtime arrangements or whatever, that they "didn't realise". Avoiding discrimination means taking positive steps. If all of us who work alongside a person with autism make every effort to be aware of what challenges that person, to get to know him or her and to facilitate opportunities to communicate, very often difficulties can be overcome. All that is needed is an awareness, a willingness ... and a bit of imagination.

Going 'part time'

One of the easiest ways to adapt to meet the needs of a person with autism is simply to reduce the time demanded. It makes perfect sense that, if a person with autism is having to work twice as hard as his neuro-typical colleague to simply manage the school or work environment, giving him a bit more time and space could be the obvious answer. Unfortunately, it is an answer that is not always explored as fully as it might be. Part-time attendance in schools as part of a full time education is perfectly legal. This option is explored in more detail in my book *Autism and Flexischooling, a shared classroom and homeschooling approach (Jessica Kingsley Publishers, 2012).*

A more common solution offered in schools tends to be where the pupil with autism attends the usual timetabled lessons for some of the time, and for the rest is taught in a removal unit, perhaps in a small group or one to one. This also can work well for the pupil, although it can be difficult and expensive to maintain.

Each of these options may be extremely helpful for a pupil with autism, since it gives a balance between 'managing' the socially demanding and often confusing world of school and allowing quieter time in a more autism-friendly environment. It allows the pupil to deal with school in manageable 'chunks', while still having time to repair, and to learn in a way that is more suitable to him or to her. It may be that a child with autism struggles so hard with the social and physical demands of school that academic learning suffers, and that allowing access to individual learning, either one to one or indeed through individual study, may be far more effective. It also allows time to explore the issues and difficulties that the school part of the week may throw up. The problems of full-time schooling may be exacerbated by the 'steamroller' effect, where there is seldom time to explore the reasons why something may have gone wrong, let alone come up with ideas of ways to make it better. Flexischooling allows time and space in an individual's 'education' to explore the autism, to find out what it means to that person and how he or she is going to learn to manage it into adulthood. An education that does not allow significant opportunity for this is likely to fall short of what a child with autism most needs.

Anders is five. He attends his local primary school for three mornings each week. On the other two mornings he is following a specialised autism program arranged at home with tutors. In the afternoons he plays with his mother and little sister. The school report that Anders is managing much better now that he is on these short morning sessions, and that he seems happy and relaxed even though he seldom joins in with activities. They are working now with the autism tutors to encourage him in very specific steps. Anders relationship with both his mother and his little sister have improved and he is becoming more ready to interact with them and more expressively affectionate.

Libby is ten and is in the final year of primary school. She attends school for approximately half the week, on a timetable that is agreed with the school each half term. Her mother is a teacher, and Libby is achieving well academically through home study. In addition, her mother reports that formal home lessons have been a 'way in' to a relationship with her daughter who was otherwise aloof and difficult to engage. At school Libby's targets are all social ones — to sit quietly in class, to work in a small group, to wait until it is her turn to give an answer, to join in with games activities. School and home work closely together to provide motivation, agreeing an on-going reward system for achieving each small target.

Saul is fifteen and attends his local large secondary school. He attends all timetabled lessons in Maths and Science, together with some other subjects as they fit in with his timetable. If an unsuitable lesson is timetabled for a session he is in school (for example, if he has a Maths lesson, then French and then Science in a morning), he attends the Pupil Support Unit instead of French. On any morning or afternoon session where he is not timetabled for either Maths or Science, he works from home. He *struggles with English and has a one to one tutor engaged by his parents. On the other hand, both his Maths and Science attainment is well above average. He completes additional on-line assignments in these at a level well beyond his age and is planning to continue them to 'A' and indeed degree level. He is also a keen swimmer and is a member of the local youth squad, attending sessions at least four times a week. He has the time (and capacity) to do this because he can prepare before each session by having quiet time by himself.*

How flexischooling is managed can be as varied as the children with autism themselves. Sometimes it is a way of allowing access to academic study. Sometimes school attendance is purely to encourage social involvement. Sometimes flexischooling is as simple as allowing a day 'off' midweek to allow the pupil to repair and to work more quietly from home. When it works, flexischooling can be a respectful alternative for the pupil with autism which allows for all of his needs to be met.

There are many ways that a working environment can reflect the flexischool approach. Unfortunately, flexible working conditions are often only offered to the higher-achieving type jobs, and if a person with autism fails to get on in the lower ranks, this practice may never be available to him.

In Grete's example given earlier, it was understood both that she would leave early on a Friday, and that she needed some time, some weeks, to work from home. This met her needs well, and her work continued at an exceptionally good level. Imagine, though, if the differentiations to allow for her autism were withdrawn. Imagine if she had to attend the Friday lunchtime meetings, was reprimanded and penalised for her lateness and her 'inattention' in other meetings, was expected to stay on into Friday afternoon in spite of growing anxiety and was denied the possibility of working from home when she needed to. It is more than possible that Grete's exemplary working record would soon be tarnished, and indeed it is quite possible that, if forced into work when feeling unable to do so, she would take the only other option and resign. Often, flexible working conditions are seen as a reward or a 'perk' when for the person with autism they may in fact be a necessity.

Part time work itself may be an answer for many people with autism, but it does carry an inherent difficulty – as well as having significant economic implications for that person. In the flexischooling example, the responsibility for making the practice work was shared between school and parent, but not left to the person with autism himself. Working flexibly, both setting this up and maintaining it, can require considerable skills of communication.

If you are absent from work for two days each week, how are you going to communicate what you have done, what needs doing in your absence, and how are you going to understand what has been going on while you were away? If something in the flexible working arrangement is seen as not working, who is going to make sure that it is put right, rather than just abandoned?

One of the best answers to helping a person with autism into employment may well be providing a job-share, particularly if the job-share partner is also the person's mentor. Clearly, this needs to be a more-than-usual arrangement, but if the mentoring and supporting element of the work is understood, respected and, indeed, rewarded then this can work very well. The job-share partner understands the need to facilitate communication, and is given the time and skills to allow for this communication to take place. He or she is able to differentiate for the person with autism, to utilise that persons skills and strengths but nevertheless be on hand to compensate for any weaknesses. The range of the work can be shared out between the two parties in a way that best suits each individual, and because two people are handling the work, any difficulties or problems should be picked up on early before they escalate.

Another element of the flexischooling model that can be transferred to the world of work is that of working from home. Saul was able to access education through on-line study, and increasingly many areas of work and employment can be managed on-line. Computer-based communication can often be a great deal easier for the person with autism than face-to-face communication, and a working world that is managed through email and via a computer desktop can be a great deal easier for him to access. The environment of home is known and secure, alleviating many of the physical demands of the workplace, and there is no need for the person to experience a possibly challenging journey. Although few jobs may be solely home-based, an option of working from home at various points in the week may be a huge boon for the person with autism. The different ways of how the person with autism can be helped to reduce the fully 'in' aspect of school or work are as many as people with autism themselves. As a way of helping those people to access either school or work, though, it is an invaluable element to take into consideration.

Managing communication

The importance of managing communication has already been touched on. Clearly, if a person has a diagnosed difficulty in social language and social communication, finding a way to overcome this difficulty is going to be paramount.

One of the most essential elements in arranging a successful school experience for the pupil with autism is communication. If his parents tell him one thing, then the teacher tells him something else, his Teaching Assistant disagrees and finally the pupil who sits next to him contradicts again, is it surprising that the child with autism experiences meltdown?

Giles finds break times at his new school very difficult, and his mother and teacher have negotiated that he spend these times, at least until he has settled, in the library. Before he leaves for school his mother reassures him that he will not have to go out into the yard at 'play time'. When morning break begins his teacher dismisses the rest of the class and tells Giles that he may go to the library. When he gets there, he finds that the music teacher is giving a lesson and he is not allowed in. He stands outside the door, unsure of what to do next. He is found here by a teaching assistant who asks why he is not outside. When Giles is unable to answer she insists that he go out into the playground. Almost inevitably, later on during break time Giles is in trouble for kicking out at another pupil.

In this example there is clearly a communication breakdown between class teacher, music teacher and teaching assistant, all of whom should have been more consistent. For Giles, though, it is quite probably that the blame will seem to be with his mother, who told him a 'lie'. It is very easy to lose confidence in the adults you are supposed to trust when what they say is not what happens.

Communication in all busy establishments is difficult but for the person with autism it is particularly important that it works. Nor should the pupil with autism have to rely on his own verbal communication, which he may find very difficult. In schools or workplaces, written communication often works better. If, for example, Giles had been given a written permission slip to be in the library he might either have been allowed in, in spite of the music lesson, or would have had a written explanation of his predicament to show to the teaching assistant. These 'permission slips' are essential. If a pupil has been given permission to do something out of the ordinary, whether it be stay in at break, leave class early, wear a different uniform or leave school early, it is essential that he can prove this to be the case if challenged. It is unfair to expect him to be able to explain his case when almost inevitably the reason he is doing something different is because he finds the situation already challenging.

Hussain carries an Autism Alert card, issued by the National Autistic Society, that explains his condition. He is able to present this card whenever he finds himself in a difficult situation, whether in school, on public transport or in any environment where he is unknown. When he was a witness to a road accident he became very distressed, not by the accident itself but by the crowd and by the fact that the policeman would not allow him to leave to catch his bus. However, once he remembered to present the card the policeman was able to understand the reasons for his distress. Hussain was allowed to wait quietly with a WPC some way away, and he was allowed to phone his father who reassured him that he would come and collect him, and that Hussain should wait where he was.

These Autism Alert Cards are available through the NAS. Additionally, some police forces offer a similar scheme called Pegasus which enables a person with communication difficulties to be registered on a database to be accessed in times of emergency. Both of these are well worth investigating.

In a work situation it may be a great deal easier for a person with autism if communication is presented visually. This might mean anything from that the tasks for the day being presented in picture form to there being a written timetable for events, but it is often the case that clarity, and a visual reference, can help a person with autism enormously. In addition, most visual forms of communication are likely to be easier in that they involve fewer social elements. Although there is a social etiquette in the sending of emails and texts, this is relatively easy to learn and copy. It is certainly less complex than the many demands of face-to-face communication, or the sometimes difficult to follow demands of the telephone.

Dealing with crisis

It is amazing with autism how quickly, and how completely, things can go wrong! In school this can lead to escalating trouble, often ending in exclusion, and in the work place it can lead to either dismissal or to the person choosing to leave the job as being the only way out of an impossible situation. If these crises can be prevented it is so much more likely that the person with autism can have success at school and work. So how can they be avoided?

The crisis is usually a severe infringement of the rules. Perhaps the person has shouted and 'lost control', perhaps he has actually lashed out at a teacher or at a fellow employee, perhaps he has merely been 'breaking the rules' and has finally been caught. Whatever has happened, it is important first of all to try to understand the situation from the person with autism's viewpoint.

Natalie was dismissed from her job as a hairdressing general assistant when she failed to attend for work for over a week and gave no explanation. When the salon rang home after she had been absent for six days, Natalie's mother reported that Natalie had left for work on time each morning and returned home on time each evening. She had given no indication that she had not gone to work, and her location was a mystery as she carried very little money. Natalie had become worried because she had been reading the hazard notices on the bottles of chemicals used for dying hair. She was worried about the instructions that products must not be allowed to touch skin and was frightened to handle the bottles. Part of her job was to tidy the trolleys after each customer, and this included disposing of the used chemical bottles.

Because she was so frightened of handling the chemicals Natalie 'escaped' by avoiding going to work. She caught her usual bus into town, using her bus pass. She then caught another bus which took her on a round trip taking a number of hours. She was then able to catch her usual bus home. In this way she stayed safe, dry and reasonably warm and did not have to use any money. She had not dared to tell her mother, who she thought would be angry with her for not going to work.

In this example Natalie's mother did not try to get her back into the job, since it seemed that the very nature of it was unsuitable. She did do considerable work with Natalie about communicating her worries and about being honest about what she was doing!

There is a curious dignity about Natalie's solution. She is, in fact, 'keeping herself safe'. She believes the job to be hazardous, and is basing this belief on realistic criteria (the safety information given on the bottles). She knows that she must find somewhere that is a safe alternative, and the bus is not a bad option. Realistically, what else could she have done?

If Natalie had had a mentor to whom she could have turned perhaps her worries could have been addressed. If the hazards of the chemicals could have been weighed up properly and scientifically it may well have been possible to reassure Natalie that she was not in any danger. Indeed, it may have been the case that she was in danger if she were not given correct protective clothing, and perhaps the situation could have been resolved by issuing her with proper protective gloves. If she had merely asked for these, however, there was every chance that she would be ridiculed or refused or both.

It takes someone with considerable social and communication skills to challenge authority successfully, and Natalie was aware that she did not have these.

It is possible in this example to see also how the problem could have escalated if Natalie had not managed it for herself. Given her level of fear regarding the bottles it is quite possible that she could have over-reacted in front of a customer perhaps even going into melt-down if, for example, the chemicals became spilt. It is also, sadly, possible to see how Natalie could have been vulnerable to bullying should her fellow workers have decided to use her fear maliciously against her. In this situation 'teasing' of the kind of flicking water at Natalie and pretending it was chemical in order to provoke a reaction would quite likely result in a violent response from Natalie which would seem to be out of all proportion. Had she hit out at a co-worker it is unlikely that her behaviour would be understood to be in genuine self-defence, even though to Natalie it would be precisely that.

The person with autism faces a different and often much more frightening world than does the neuro-typical person. In both school and work it is important that there is someone who has the time and the understanding to support the person when they hit a problem or difficulty, before that problem escalates and gets more serious. It is also essential that the person with autism is protected against malice and bullying, to which he is likely to be only too vulnerable. Above all, should a crisis occur it is essential that the situation is looked at with an eye to the person with autism's perspective. The person's behaviour may appear to be disproportionate or to make no sense, but it will make sense, and be in proportion to that person.

Inclusion and differentiation mean allowing for the autism, even in a crisis situation. If the crisis has happened because the school or workplace have not put sufficient support in place to help that person with autism to manage, then it is very unfair if the person with autism is the one who has to accept all the responsibility.

Being part of the 'team'

The best support for a person with autism, whether child or adult, is provided by a team of people. This might include parents, staff, autism outreach worker, disability support workers, other pupils, co-workers and, most importantly, the person with autism himself. This team approach allows everyone involved to see the potential pitfalls of autism as challenges to be met and overcome, and all value the person with autism as someone who is worth helping. This positive approach allows the person to request help, sure in the knowledge that there will be people around him who can, and who are happy to, provide that advice and assistance. Often this help will be very practical. If we look back at the first section of this book ("What is autism?") we can see that many of the ways to help a person with autism to overcome the disabling aspects of their condition are to do with helping them to be organised. Someone who has problems with Central Coherence (seeing the 'big picture') and Executive Functioning (organising what, where and when) is going to be helped by being supported to be ordered and in control. Often this sort of support is very easy to put into place and it can be immensely satisfying to see just how much difference it can make to the person.

Tom's schoolbooks are all marked with a small, colour-coded bar on the spines. This corresponds to the colour-coding on his timetable and on his map of the school. On his locker keyring he carries a series of small laminated coloured key fobs. These correspond to his lessons for the day.

In this way, Tom can see by reference to his key fobs that the next lesson will be science (blue) in the science lab (blue on the timetable). When he gets to the lesson he knows to take out the books with the blue spine bar, and to check in the blue section of his file for homework to be handed in. In his homework diary he has a blue cross against the day, so he knows to expect homework and where to write it.

This 'invisible' support can be a tremendous boost to independence. Not only does it allow Tom to manage without having the rather obvious support of an adult with him, but it teaches him strategies to use into later life. By organising him now his parents and support workers are giving him the skills he needs to learn to organise himself when he grows up.

Magnus is twinned with a 'buddy' at his work cleaning offices. This buddy, who varies from shift to shift, knows to set Magnus' timer at the start of each room. If left to himself Magnus would continue to clean each office until it was fully clean to his satisfaction (which might never happen!). The timer indicates to Magnus how long he should take on each office and when it is time to move on.

Very often the problems that a task involves for a person with autism lie in interpreting what is really wanted. In Magnus' case this is to do with how long he should take on each section. In a pupil's case it might be to do with how much detail is required in an answer or what the real purpose of an activity is. Organisational supports such as providing a box on worksheets that give an indication of how much writing is required can be a tremendous help, as can having someone who is able to help a pupil with autism to prioritise. It may be that you do not know the date to fill in at the top of the exam paper, but that should not stop you from carrying on with an exam once the time has started! Equally, the neuro-typical pupil can usually tell the difference between 'important' work and extension work that has been set as a way of occupying the class, perhaps while other students catch up or because the teacher doesn't want to start a new topic at that stage of the term. Having a member of the pupil's autism team who is able to indicate this difference to a pupil with autism can prevent a great deal of frustration and wasted effort. Some schools have the excellent system of using Sixth Formers as mentors for more vulnerable children lower down the school. In this case this would be the ideal person to interpret for the pupil which tasks need doing properly, taking the majority of the pupil's allotted time, and which might be approached more superficially.

Whether the people with autism in your life are friends or family, whether work colleagues, classmates, parents, children or siblings, helping to develop a team support network, and being ready to be a member of that team yourself, is a great step towards helping them to manage their lives and their condition. Having autism can be an intrinsically lonely experience. Difficulties with social interaction, communication and imagination must feel like a wall between you and all those neuro-typical others who speak an unknown language, who understand what is not said and can seem to read each other's minds. If we can each of us be part of the teams that support these people, that accept them, respect them, like and love them, then how far we can go to at least starting to knock down that wall!

****

Conclusion: So why this book?

For many people with autism the experiences of life may not feel like successful ones. As those people who were first diagnosed with autism grow up, many of them are able to articulate just how distressing their experiences are. Many, for example, found school very difficult indeed. Some were overtly bullied, by pupils and sometimes by staff. Others speak of feeling isolated and alone and unable to make sense of the world around them. Many failed to achieve academically, and even as adults continue to believe that they 'cannot do'. If they have failed at work – been unable to secure it, been dismissed when they have found it or been forced to leave because it was all too difficult – this self perception as someone who cannot succeed can be further reinforced. Many people with autism report depression and anxiety, and for many the diagnosis has not been the liberating key that it might have been. Sure, it explains, finally, why they 'cannot do' so many things, but it does not help to turn this around into a way of overcoming and of finding success.

This book tries to at least begin to explain autism to the non-autistic majority. It tries to give an insight into exactly what the condition is and what it means for the people who experience it. If the purpose was solely to 'explain why things are so awful for people with autism', then frankly I don't think it would have been worth writing. But it is not. Part of understanding autism is to realise ways to help. This helping is not with the autism, but is helping the people who have autism to manage the problems that having autism throw up for them. There is nothing intrinsically bad or sad about having autism. Having autism can and does make some situations bad and difficult, it can make the person sad, anxious, depressed and angry ... but it is NOT hopeless!

One of the biggest steps we can all take, whether we have autism ourselves or not, is to accept people with autism. Once we recognise the autism spectrum and can understand something of what it means to the person we are in a position to accept it in the people we meet. We know a little of how to be sensitive to that person's needs. We understand some of that person's behaviours and are ready not to be offended or put off by them and we can begin to see past the problems of the condition to the person – funny, bright, ordinary, kind, original, quirky – who has the autism.

Sam was asked who his friends were at school. He replied, "I have none." At the beginning of Year Five, he decided to stand in the upcoming school council elections. His parents tried their best to dissuade him, fearing further damage to his already fragile self esteem. They discussed the matter with his class teacher, who shared their concern but who was able to reassure them that the ballot was secret and the results were not shared apart from the winner. She guaranteed that she would not let Sam face humiliation. Both she and Sam's parents spent some time trying to prepare him for the day of the results, explaining that a great many pupils were standing and how hard it was to be elected. They were aware that most children would vote for their friends and knew that Sam could not even name another pupil in his class.

Sam won the election by a 'land slide'. His peers, when questioned, were able to identify all of the positives in his autism. They said that he was trustworthy and that he would take the job seriously. They said that he wouldn't take sides and that he wouldn't be swayed to only represent certain 'cliques' in the class. They said that he would be keenly alert for injustice and that he would not be afraid to raise their concerns with adults. They said that he would keep focussed on an issue until it was resolved and would never 'give up'. They mentioned his extremely good memory, his attention to detail, his advanced reading skills and his well-organised approach.

When asked again who his friends were, Sam replied, "I have lots of friends. I don't know who they are, but they are all around me."

Sam is our son.

****

Appendix: An Autism Directory

One thing that you are going to have to get your head around, as you become involved in the world of autism, is a whole new vocabulary. The following is far from exhaustive, but it does give some easy-to-understand interpretations of some of the many words and phrases that you are likely to encounter. Please bear in mind that many of the definitions, if explored fully, would merit a book in their own right – so these are only the very briefest and most simplistic 'thumb-nail' sketches!

ADOS: Autism Diagnostic Observation Schedule. A set of observations and conclusions often used in the diagnosis of ASD.

ADD/ADHD: Attention Deficit Disorder and Attention Deficit Hyperactivity Disorder. Separate conditions that may exist alongside autism. Need to be diagnosed (and treated) separately as some aspects of ASD may look like ADD/ADHD when, in fact, they are not.

Amygdala: the part of the brain thought to process emotions. Some researchers believe that this may be differently structured in people with ASD.

Cognitive Behavioural Therapy: psychological technique that teaches about emotions and emotional responses using a conscious and analytical approach.

Central Coherence: the ability to see the 'big picture'. It may be that some people with autism are very good at seeing the detail, but poor at organising that information to create meaning. (Weak central coherence is now sometimes called 'monotropism'.)

Cognitive ability: intellectual ability. IQ (Intelligence Quotient) tests measure a person's so-called 'raw intelligence'. The scale gives an average score of 100, with roughly 50% of the population scoring between 90 and 110. Any score above 70 is taken to be in the 'normal range' (ie the person is not described as Learning Disabled.) A person with autism is likely to have an unusual profile of cognitive ability – to be poor at some things, and good at others. It is important that a person is aware of his cognitive 'style' so that he gets the help he needs where he needs it and (perhaps even more importantly) he can be fully aware of where his strengths are.

DSM-5: 5th and current Diagnostic and Statistical Manual of Mental Disorders, published in 2013. This manual is used to decide the precise classification of various disorders, including Autism Spectrum Disorder.

Dyspraxia, dyslexia, dyscalculia: all describe problems with planning and management of various things: movement and language, reading and writing, mathematics. Any or all may be evident in people with autism, although all can be explored as separate conditions.

Echolalia: the repeating of words or phrases back to the speaker. Some people with ASD can quote whole scenes from DVDs or television programmes or from what has been heard on the radio, apparently without effort and without connection to the content.

Executive function: the ability to self organise, prioritise, understand the significance of different materials, plan and predict. This ability to 'sort out what to do' may be significantly delayed or impaired in people with autism.

Gifted, talented and more able: May be used to describe

children with an IQ above 130 (top 2% of the population), or more generally to describe the most 'able' children in a school or district. People with autism may feature in either category.

Hyperlexia: advanced ability to decode words in reading. However, understanding of content, context or storyline may lag behind.

Irlen lenses: System of tinted lenses designed to help with visual sensitivities and processing difficulties in autism and other conditions.

Macrocephalus: having a larger than usual head. There is some evidence that this may be more common than usual in children with autism.

Neologism: the making up of new words. This is one of the more charming aspects of some children's autism and you may find that these new names for things become part of your family's 'vocabulary' for generations to come!

Neurotypical: people without autism. Some 'Aspie' groups refer to this group as NTs in response to NTs referring to them as having AS. Other people prefer terms such as the Predominant Neurotype, since not all people who do not have autism and neuro-typical.

OCD: Obsessive Compulsive Disorder. Obsessive thoughts that lead to obsessive, repetitive actions in a cycle that the person cannot break. So, for example, the person may have obsessive thoughts about dirt, repeatedly need to wash hands and become anxious and distressed if unable to do so. OCD is not a symptom of ASD, but people with autism may be particularly vulnerable to developing OCD.

Prosopagnosia: face blindness. A person with autism may not be able to recognise individuals (our son could not recognise me from the other parents when we first sent him to school and had to be told by his teacher which one I was!). Face blindness also means that the person struggles to interpret facial expressions, so the person may not know when someone is joking or becoming angry.

Sensory Integration Therapy: developed by occupational therapists to help regulate sensory differences in children with autism. Children balance, swing, roll and are squashed using deep pressure.

Theory of Mind: the ability to empathise, to understand a person's thoughts from their perspective.

Visual cues: ways to help a person with autism in a non-verbal way. They can be anything from a picture of a sandwich to prompt the person to go to have lunch to a box drawn on a worksheet to indicate where the answer should go. They can include a timer to indicate when an activity will change, a 'red card' to indicate that the person's behaviour is about to get them into trouble, a reward token to be put towards time playing on the computer, for example, or a post-it note to remind the person to make a phone call. Visual cues seem to help many people with autism, even those at the most 'high functioning' end of the spectrum, and they can be one answer to how to manage living together with someone with autism in greater harmony!

****